MORE THAN PETTICOATS

Remarkable Illlinois Women

DATE DUE

MORE THAN PETTICOATS SERIES

MORE THAN PETTICOATS

Remarkable Illinois Women

Lyndee Jobe Henderson

TWODOT®

GUILFORD, CONNECTICUT
HELENA, MONTANA
AN IMPRINT OF THE GLOBE PEQUOT PRESS

A · **TWODOT**® · **BOOK**

Copyright © 2007 by Morris Book Publishing, LLC

Text design by Nancy Freeborn
Map by M. A. Dubé © Morris Book Publishing, LLC

Library of Congress Cataloging-in-Publication Data
Henderson, Lyndee Jobe.
  More than petticoats. Remarkable Illinois women/Lyndee Jobe Henderson.—
1st ed.
       p. cm.—(More than petticoats series)
  Includes bibliographical references.
  ISBN-13: 978-0-7627-1271-7
  ISBN-10: 0-7627-1271-6
  1. Women—Illinois—Biography. 2. Women—Illinois—History. 3. Illinois—
Biography. I. Title. II. Title: Remarkable Illinois women.
  CT3262.I5H46 2007
  920.0773—dc22

                                                                 2006017689

Manufactured in the United States of America
First Edition/First Printing

CONTENTS

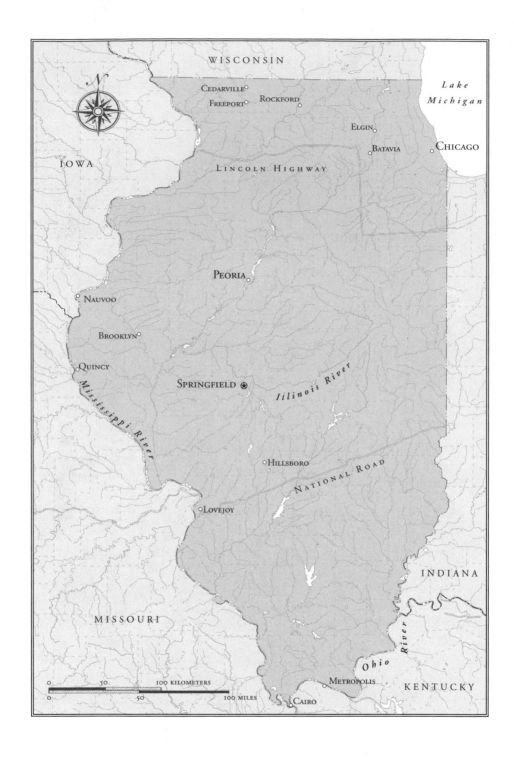

ILLINOIS

ACKNOWLEDGMENTS

Help comes in many forms, and this project required the aid of dozens of people over a period of four long years. To those nameless individuals who kindly answered the phone, or took my written request, or made a suggestion, or shared an idea, I thank you!

I am especially indebted to the archivists at the Chicago History Museum; to the research librarians at the Harold Washington Library; to Iris Nelson, Quincy historian and research librarian; to the staff at the Quincy Public Library; to the Historical Society of Quincy and Adams County; to the staff at the Special Collections Department at Bradley University; to the Peoria Historical Society; to the research librarians at the Peoria Public Library; to the staff and research librarians at the Naperville Public Library; to the research librarians at the Monroe County Library (New York), including the staff and research librarians at the Rochester Public Library, the Fairport Public Library, and the Pittsford Public Library. Thanks also to Quincy historian Shirley Landrum and Mr. William McLaughlin.

Sincere thanks to my cheerleaders: to Ellyn and Brett Edmonds; to Ross and Jennifer Henderson; to R. Dean and Phyllis Jobe; and to author, artist, and friend Lisa Patti Konkol for providing advice and critique.

I would also like to thank my faithful editor, Stephanie Hester, for trusting me to pick up the ball and start running again. I especially want to thank my husband Larry who provided endless technical support and patience throughout this process.

INTRODUCTION

"Let me do all the good I can while I stay." It was the deathbed sentiment of Myra Bradwell, but words that might have been said by any one of the twelve women in this book. Although each came from different experiences and backgrounds, they all shared a common life theme: service to others.

It might be easy to say their actions stemmed from the philosophies of Puritanism or True Womanhood. Both revolved around the idea that a virtuous woman should live in devotion to others. Yet, there is no sense that these women were consciously following a set of guidelines. Some were religious, some struggled with theology. It seems instead that they were driven by instinct, passion, and love.

The women herein were born over a span of more than one hundred years, from 1796 to 1899. Their stories are eerily similar: many lost their children to illnesses that today would be considered common and curable; they escaped poverty and worked with seemingly endless stamina toward building a better life; and although they repeatedly withstood crushing disappointments, deaths of loved ones, and unspeakable grief, they persevered.

Several took on enormous projects with the attitude of "when" rather than "if" it would come to fruition. None were driven by a quest for fame. When the telegram arrived announcing that she had won the Nobel Peace Prize, Jane Addams read it and then placed it in her bureau drawer, keeping the news a secret from all but one nephew. Mary Todd Lincoln enjoyed the perks of being first lady, but there is no doubt that had she been given the choice to change the defining moments of her life, she would have given up all and asked for the restoration of her lost children and beloved husband.

True, several were openly proud, but they tempered that emotion with modesty. And although these women accomplished more in one year than many of us do in a lifetime, they did so with an air of casualness. Lydia Moss Bradley wrote a $1 million check to cover the construction bill for the college buildings bearing her name, and then pulled on her boots and went to her garden to cut flowers for the dinner table. Candace Reed walked away from a lucrative photography business to assist as a nurse during the Civil War. These women showed no hesitation when it came to sacrifices made for the benefit of the community at large.

As a strong believer that people are molded by virtue of their roots, the place from which they came and the early relationship between a parent and child, I was especially intrigued by their formative childhood years. Annie Malone was the daughter of freed slaves, but it was her experience as an orphan that moved her to donate generously to children's homes. The deep religiosity of the Hale household unwittingly laid the foundation for Emma Hale Smith's life as a missionary and wife of the founder of the Mormon Church. And Irene Castle's fight against vivisection emanated from her childhood love of dogs, horses, and an array of other pets.

The era in which these women lived was ever changing. Despite limited innovation in the fields of communication and transportation, they managed to travel across the country, and in some cases, the world, without the conveniences that have made those endeavors much easier with the passage of time. Christiana Tillson lived long enough to witness dramatic changes and improvements. Reading her comments from a modern perspective, I was struck by the humor of her reminding her daughter that she should be grateful for the ease of her 1870s lifestyle. Of course, everyone's experience is relative: If you don't know what you're missing, how can you yearn for it?

It is a monumental task to condense the life of a woman into about 3,000 words. A cottage industry of sorts has evolved around

Jane Addams, who has been dissected and analyzed through decades of scholarly writings that cover all aspects of her thinking, from sociology, to theology, to pacifism and socialism—not to mention her personal life. Ruth Page intended to write just one book, yet managed to produce several, as well as maintain an extensive collection of more than 1,000 pages of notes on dances she choreographed during her seventy-year career. On the other hand, the life story of Anna Elizabeth Slough, who was a somewhat typical early Illinois resident, was uncovered in now dusty, fragile volumes containing portraits of early settlers, one small paragraph here and there, a newspaper article, an advertisement, an obituary.

On a personal note, I consider myself privileged to have had the opportunity to write about each. Their ardent devotion to others is a template for future generations. After four years of spending time with them, it was hard to say good-bye.

CHRISTIANA HOLMES TILLSON

1798-1872

Accidental Historian

COMFORTABLY PROPPED UP BY PILLOWS in the center of her feather bed, seventy-one-year-old Christiana Holmes Tillson rubbed her stiffened fingers with the palms of her hands, hoping to rejuvenate her aging joints long enough to begin writing. Finally, picking up the quill, she carefully dipped the writing instrument into the inkwell on her bed tray and placed the point on the sheet of paper. Much like writing a letter to a friend, she began:

Amherst, Mass., June 28, 1870

Dear Daughter:

Whenever you have expressed a wish that I would write out some of my early western experiences, I have felt an inclination to comply with your request. . . . As writing is not my forte, I do not feel that I can produce anything which will at present interest you much; but my own appreciation of every record left me by my good mother and my dear husband makes me feel that I may leave you something which will interest you in after life, more than at the present time.

Christiana proceeded to write a narrative that would later be called a remarkable record of the life of a pioneer woman in 1820s Illinois. The 154-page memoir, originally titled *Reminiscences of Early Life in Illinois by Our Mother,* was initially published in limited quantity and privately issued by her daughter for use within the family. Christiana died in 1872, months before the first edition was available. Although her musings described just a few years of their pioneer experiences, Christiana and John Tillson's Illinois odyssey actually spanned decades.

Both Christiana and John hailed from Massachusetts. Christiana Holmes was born in the Old Colony town of Kingston on October 11, 1798. Her family lineage contained Pilgrim and Revolutionary War stock. As was common in well-to-do New England homes, her parents provided her an honorable education, which focused on religion, reading, and writing.

John Tillson's ancestors arrived in America aboard the *Mayflower.* Two years her senior, John, with his industrious spirit and independent thinking, was well suited for Christiana. He too received a solid education and enjoyed an upper-class lifestyle.

Prior to their marriage, John accepted a job in the West, securing bounty lands for eastern speculators. Christiana must have wondered if he would ever come back. It would not be a question of love that might affect their future, but the unknown territory, which harbored danger as well as fortune for those so daring.

After nearly two years, John returned and kept his promise of marriage. The couple wed on October 6, 1822, just days before Christiana's twenty-fourth birthday. Family and friends expressed anxiety about the newlyweds moving to Illinois. Christiana wrote of her own nervousness about the trip:

CHRISTIANA HOLMES TILLSON

Partings, the breaking up of families and home attachments, have always been to me particularly painful, and the sad forebodings I was constantly hearing at that time of the fearful journey, and the dismal backwoods life which awaited me were not calculated to dispel the clouds that would sometimes come over me.

With a heavy heart and understandable reservation, she assumed the carriage seat beside her new husband, and the pair began their wedded life embarking on the same excursion west that had been made by thousands before them.

Along the way, the young bride experienced some disappointments. Her New York City honeymoon was abbreviated when it was discovered the residents there were suffering a yellow fever epidemic. Another letdown came when they finally reached St. Louis. At the port, Christiana fully expected to claim several cartons containing her belongings, which had been shipped two weeks ahead of their Massachusetts departure. The Tillsons were told that the New Orleans–based boat carrying their treasures was probably lost. The fall winds already chilled the air, and since her winter clothing was among the lost parcels, Christiana was forced to purchase a ready-made dress and yards of blue and white check fabric for another to be constructed by a city tailor. The next concern was replacing household goods.

The price of furniture in St. Louis was quite steep. As luck would have it, a local widow was dispensing of her estate and, in what might be considered a nineteenth-century yard sale, the Tillsons purchased several nice items to outfit their residence. Finally, it was time for the ride to their prairie home.

The weariness Christiana felt from the nearly two-month journey and the loss of her possessions must have been magnified when her new wilderness home came into view. The meager bachelor's den that her husband had kept before his marriage sat in lonely stead on a large parcel. It was a far cry from the type of architecture and community she had grown up in back in Massachusetts. Christiana searched for joys within the log house walls during that first evening in their marital home. As a woman used to a lifestyle that included nice things, she commented with humor about the haphazard array of candles that she found waiting for her in the one-room cabin:

Four large nails with their points driven into a square block of wood served as one candlestick, the other was supplied by paper being wound around the candle and then inserted into the neck of a glass bottle; this made quite a display.

Almost immediately, Christiana realized that she was a novelty among the locals. After all, she was a Yankee! Curious neighbors stopped by to evaluate the new Mrs. Tillson. It became apparent that class envy was rampant in prairie Illinois.

Eastern settlers were typically well-to-do; the long trip west required substantial funds. They often arrived in Baltimore carriages pulled by handsome horses. Yankee retailers were suspect for selling goods at outlandish prices.

On the other hand, those migrating from the South were often poor and white, traveling by foot, wearing inadequate clothing, and owning few possessions. Banking on securing land as squatters, most southern immigrants were farmers who labored on large farms for pay and then came home to plough and harvest their own land.

The term "poor white folk" was just as much a slur to their neighbors as being called a Yankee was to the Tillsons. Christiana defended her use of the phrase, writing:

Perhaps I should explain that "white folks" was a name given in derision to the first emigrants from the western and southern states. An old Tennessee woman who had a terrific opinion of the

Yankees, said; "I am getting skerry about them 'ere Yankees; there is such a power of them coming in that they and the Injuns will squatch out all the white folks." Nothing afterward would exasperate them more than to have a Yankee call them white folks.

Uniquely, Christiana recorded the conversations of white folks using their dialect. She also reported on the uncomfortable reactions of her new neighbors. One woman was shocked when Christiana offered her a slice of her homemade Yankee pie. The fact that Christiana would use the word "Yankee" in front of her was surprising, and the woman responded, "I didn't think you would say the like of that; I allus knowed youens were all Yankees, but Billy said 'Don't let on that we know it, kase it'll jest make them mad.'"

Everything at the Tillson residence seemed scrutinized. Even Christiana's laundry drew an audience as she chose the New England method of hanging it from a line using clothespins, unlike her neighbors who pitched their wet clothes over the fence to dry. The voices were loud enough for Christiana's ears, and as one man marveled, "See here, ain't that jest the last Yankee fixin'? Jest see them ar little boys ridin' on a rope."

Christiana was quickly introduced to a variety of customs not practiced back home. One major annoyance was the expected hospitality toward unexpected Sunday guests. At the time, proper decorum prevented her from closing her door to callers. However, in her journal she complained fiercely about the weekly "legion of visitors," mainly because of the amount of work it took to feed them.

Back east, the Tillsons would have kept the Sabbath as a day of rest. In Illinois, the lack of churches and the expectations of the uninvited interfered with Christiana's private reading time and religious ritual. Christiana used these visits to study the manners of each person who walked into her home. Most spoke with a southern drawl. The men were brawny and not all together clean. The women wore a simple bonnet, but no coat even in winter. They kept track of the youngsters, and nursed without proper cover-up. At times, Christiana noticed that the women cowered when their husbands spoke. Christiana wrote that a man in this western culture could control his wife in lieu of a slave.

The interlopers were often odd and suspicious in nature, and sometimes they rudely opened Christiana's cabinets and closets to see what she owned. Many thought her dinnerware was for sale since she had so many pieces lined on the shelves.

It was expected that the Tillsons would visit their neighbors in return on another Sunday. Christiana cleverly circumvented the tradition by taking John on mid-week return visits. This upset the unprepared hosts, as it interrupted the wife's daily chores and startled the husband, who, after a long day in the fields, was unhappy to find the Tillsons sitting in their kitchen, prepared to chat and eat. The message circulated that if you stopped by the Yankees, they might visit you on the wrong day. The Sabbath knocks on the Tillsons' door subsided.

When spring arrived the Tillsons were eagerly anticipating the birth of a child, the first of three, due later in the year. They were also delighted to learn that their boxes were miraculously at port after having sat all winter on a boat that required repairs. The break in weather also meant that they could begin expansion of their log home to include a parlor and a bedroom. Neighbors now declared that the Tillsons "had a power of room and were power down well fixed." Christiana wrote that considering the animosity between the poor white folks and the Yankees, she was surprised that she and her husband enjoyed a peaceful relationship with them.

One aspect of prairie life that affected all citizens equally was the lack of medical care. When John fell seriously ill with a high fever, Christiana had no choice but to serve as his nurse. The closest doctor lived a full day's ride away and when called upon, he lingered until the patient improved. Christiana shared her tremendous fears as John teetered in and out of consciousness:

> I had to carry him through a course of treatment the best I could, though with fearful forebodings as to whether I was pursuing the right course. The anxiety and responsibility I felt about his sickness was more than all the labor and care with which I was burdened.

By the time the doctor arrived, Christiana had stayed by John's bed for more than a week. The doctor commended her skill and she rejoiced: "A heavy responsibility had been lifted from my poor, tired-out body and mind."

The episode shook Christiana. A Yankee lady friend heard about the Tillsons' plight and traveled a great distance to offer her assistance. Christiana gratefully accepted:

> To those who have never known the loneliness that had encircled me for the past few weeks, my feelings could not be described. . . . Such friends and such acts of friendship can never be forgotten, nor can they be understood by those who have not been in like isolation.

As an educated woman in a society that frowned on girls attending school, Christiana admitted that she "had some ambition to show off a little, being aware that the white folks though very friendly when I met them, were much perplexed to know what Tillson's wife found to do." Christiana wasn't known to farm, and to outsiders she didn't appear to be much of a housewife. When the opportunity presented itself, Christiana demonstrated her usefulness.

On a day when John was traveling, a local businessman named Mr. Roundtree called to settle his accounts. Discovering Christiana home alone, Roundtree used a patronizing tone to request the books for review. Christiana not only produced the books but transcribed his bills into them and completed the math, much to his amazement. He declared, "Why I had no idea you were such a scribe . . . and you have made the charges correctly." No doubt, little time was spared before news circulated about Mrs. Tillson's business skills.

In an era and culture where a proper woman deferred to the decisions of her husband, John and Christiana shared ideas and opinions as a marital team. John's work required he cross dangerously unpredictable creeks in the daylight and darkness, and Christiana fretted about him navigating a safe passage home. One night they discussed moving closer to John's business in Hillsboro.

At his suggestion, they collaborated on plans to construct what would be the first brick home built in Montgomery County. Completed in 1827, the Homestead became a landmark of hospitality to travelers as well as a spacious residence. Yet, the decor was modest, as the Tillsons apparently attempted to tone down their wealth, living below their means to avoid upsetting their neighbors. In Christiana's own words the space was "meekly furnished to serve the demands of comfort and to avoid the censure and envy of the multitude."

Slavery was a hot topic, especially in southern Illinois where much of the population had roots in slave states. When Illinois was awarded statehood in 1818, it was designated a free state, although those who owned slaves already were permitted to retain them either as indentured servants or as slaves. The law was complicated and, as Yankees, the Tillsons viewed the concept quite negatively. It is ironic, then, that the Tillsons became slave owners, albeit in a roundabout way.

One of John's business associates named Mr. McLaughlin owned two indentured slaves and asked if John might be interested in purchasing them. Otherwise, he intended to sell them in New

Orleans. John enjoyed Lucy's cooking and was always kind to Caleb, but he declined the offer, never anticipating that within weeks he would be inadvertently harboring Lucy and Caleb as runaways.

It was in the early morning when, following her daily routine, Christiana arose to begin cooking breakfast. Opening the kitchen door, she entered the room and nearly stepped on two "specimens of humanity stretched horizontally, covering almost the entire vacant space on our small kitchen floor." Those specimens were Lucy and Caleb. Taken aback at the sight, Christiana called for John, who immediately recognized the urgent faces in front of him. Proper protocol required that John immediately contact their owner, which he did by letter.

Lucy and Caleb asked John Tillson to reconsider keeping them on, and it just so happened that the timing of their request made him agreeable. He was aware that his wife had become over-whelmed with daily tasks. Christiana was exhausted and suffering an unknown illness that caused her hair to fall out. Now a mother, a business assistant for her husband, a store clerk, and a cook for workmen who boarded with them, she also realized that she needed help. When Mr. McLaughlin arrived with a second proposal that would convey ownership of Lucy and Caleb to the Tillsons, the idea was distasteful, yet it was a solution to ease her burden. By way of explanation, Christiana wrote:

> Nothing but dire necessity could have induced us to the course we pursued in taking them. . . . It was no small consideration with me, worn down as I was. . . . Still it was slavery—the price of blood—that haunted me.

She also felt that it was a way of saving Lucy and Caleb from an uncertain future:

I saw that your father's wish was to retain them, and as my kitchen labors were to be abated, and feeling, too, as he did, that I could not think of having them sent off to the slave pens of New Orleans, we both concluded to keep them. Work was made lighter, but conscience not quite easy.

John died suddenly on May 11, 1853. Some speculated that at the time of his death, he was Illinois's wealthiest man. His philanthropic generosities led to the establishment of Illinois colleges, churches, and public buildings. Christiana supported John's causes, writing that her husband was a "cheerful giver." She continued, "It is one of the greatest comforts to me in looking back on the past that we were placed in a condition to extend favors to others."

The Tillsons had four children. With John departed, Christiana resided in Illinois with the couple's only daughter, who was also her Christiana's namesake. The young Christiana adored her mother and lovingly served as her constant friend and living companion. Eventually, they moved east to Massachusetts and then New York.

As an elderly woman, Christiana became bedridden, suffering the chronic recurrence of rheumatism, upset stomach, and bronchial infection. Perhaps her daughter's suggestion that she write about her early years on the Illinois prairie was a way to keep her alert and active. Many of the paragraphs specifically address the younger Christiana.

Writing about events fifty years earlier, the older Christiana advised her daughter to appreciate the modern conveniences that 1870s life afforded. Apparently, the younger Christiana viewed the early days as a romantic time. Her mother set her straight, clarifying that 1820s prairie life was an everyday battle. The journal ended abruptly, two years after its start.

Upon her passing, the *Evangelist* newspaper described Christiana in its New York edition:

Her last four years of patient sickness and joyous trust in God and tenderness toward friends seemed but the perfect blossoming of a life which in itself gathered strength and beauty from many sources to meet the unusual demands upon her heart, brain, and hands; which she did with rare ability to organize and to execute.

In 1919, historian Milo M. Quaife discovered Christiana's story and introduced a slightly edited version under the title *A Woman's Story of Pioneer Illinois*. The book was offered under the imprint of Lakeside Press as part of Chicago-based R. R. Donnelly's annual Christmas promotion. Christiana's uncensored frankness and crisp descriptions made the book one of the publisher's most demanded titles.

ANNA ELIZABETH SLOUGH

ca. 1800–1878

Determined Mother

HEADSTRONG ANNA ELIZABETH SLOUGH NESTLED HER youngest child into the front seat of the single-horse carriage, then gathered her skirts by the hem and climbed into the driver's seat. Earlier, she had equipped the carriage with food and supplies to sustain them during the long trip across the mountains of Pennsylvania. It was the spring of 1832, and Anna intended to claim the 160 acres allotted to her veteran husband for his service in the War of 1812.

When Congress set aside the Military Tract, which was a 3.5 million-acre triangle of land between the Mississippi and Illinois Rivers, it was doing more than gifting land for duty performed. The underlying reason for the government's generosity was to encourage settlement in Illinois. Veterans were also offered back pay to ease the financial burden associated with securing the bounty land.

Despite the incentives, many former soldiers found it difficult to leave their family, home, and work in order to obtain their land personally. Some sold their options to speculators and pocketed the money. Others hired an agent to conduct the transaction of surveying the parcel and recording the deed. Anna considered herself more than capable of acting as the requisition agent for her spouse's claim.

With hardly a reservation about the long road ahead of her, Anna exchanged good-byes with her husband Jacob and the couple's other children, who stood by the roadside, waving farewell. She steered the carriage through the streets of Harrisburg, which had been her home since marrying Mr. Jacob Slough in Lancaster City on July 28, 1816. Here, she and Jacob had enjoyed much business success. He owned a barbershop and Anna ran a popular millinery store. The couple actively participated in the community and politics, and they had family and friends in nearby towns.

But Anna was anxious to start a new life with her family in the unknown western territory and to "grow up with the land." Driven by this golden opportunity, her ultimate goal was to secure enough land so that one day she and Jacob could divide it among their children. She realized that pursuing this dream would mean that she and Jacob would be forced to start over, but Anna was confident of her ability to build another strong business no matter where she settled. Although she knew the initial trip might be hard and possibly dangerous for a woman without benefit of a man to defend her, she felt it was a risk worth taking. This wasn't the first fantastic journey for Anna.

At the tender age of five, she accompanied her parents who immigrated to America from the German region of Saxony. Records do not provide an accurate birth date for Anna or a consistent spelling of her family name. One publication referred to her father as Cype, another as Saip, and later, in Illinois, a newspaper identified her maiden name as Seipp. Name aside, her early family life was filled with adventure. Perhaps her earlier travel experiences gave her the courage to travel to the area known as the "Far West."

Her journey began over the Allegheny Mountains, then, following the National Road, Anna crossed central Ohio to Cincinnati,

ANNA ELIZABETH SLOUGH

and into Indiana. Although passenger and freight traffic frequented the route, the highway was little more than a mixture of mud, swamp, and bogs peppered with corduroy roads. Corduroy roads were constructed of logs of varying width and dimension, placed perpendicular to the roadbed. The unpredictable surface often shifted askew from the weight and frequency of the vehicles, causing broken wagon wheels, injured horses, and settlers with sore backs. The trip was tedious at best.

It was common to sleep and eat in private homes along the trail, but accommodations were often less than ideal for a woman with a small child. Sleeping on the floor or in one tiny bed was typical. Meals consisted of feasts at some residences and bread and soup at others. At times there was hardly enough food to satisfy the appetite of a traveler hungry from battling the difficult road from dawn to dusk.

When she arrived in St. Louis, Anna hired a boat to transport the carriage along the Illinois River to the prairie town of Peoria, Illinois. Anna immediately liked the look of the land and the burgeoning town of Peoria. Since it was located next to the Illinois River, Peoria experienced rapid growth. Goods and services were much better established there than in towns located inland.

Anna began an earnest search for a business suitable for her family. She met with Mr. Eads, a businessman who was thinking of selling his two-story house overlooking the river. Anna knew the house would make a perfect hotel and tavern because of the choice location on Washington Street, near the center of town. She imagined entertaining guests, weary from their travels in the wilderness. The rushing sound of the Illinois River was relaxing, and the riverboat traffic was entertaining. The house featured upstairs sleeping rooms of reasonable size and view. From a practical sense, there was a separate room suitable for use as a bar, and the exterior was a sturdy block construction. Anna convinced Mr. Eads to sell her the property. After some wrangling, he agreed.

That accomplished, her next point of business was to acquire the land awarded to her husband for serving in the War of 1812 with the Pennsylvania Volunteers. Jacob had been recognized for his bravery during the Battle of Baltimore. Anna felt his efforts should be rewarded and quickly secured the 160 acres his patent permitted. Realizing there were independent parties eager to sell additional land, Anna again exercised her negotiating skills to buy nearly 800 additional acres near the town of Big Hollow. Her persistence and knowledge impressed locals, and her independence became the talk of the town.

In one year, Anna surpassed her goals, purchasing the block-house to be used as a residence and business, and more than 900 acres of land. Now she prepared for the return trip to Pennsylvania to retrieve Jacob and the other children. She placed the land in the care of hired help and Mr. Eads agreed to maintain the house while she was gone. The feisty Anna then packed her child and supplies into the carriage and began the cross-country trip to Pennsylvania.

Back in Harrisburg, Anna settled family and business details. Closing Jacob's barbershop and her millinery store was a slow process. Another year passed before the Sloughs were free to relocate. Finally, in 1834, they bid fond farewells to friends, family, and neighbors. Anna led the caravan to Illinois with Jacob and the children and all the household goods they could carry.

Upon their October arrival, Anna and Jacob immediately turned the Washington Street residence into a hotel. The establishment was originally named Slough's Tavern. Locals noted the Sloughs' renovation and discussed the newly pretentious exterior. Anna often stood in the front entry calling to passersby and neighbors to stop in for a bite to eat.

Anna soon developed a reputation for her outstanding abilities as a hostess. Determined to make the business a success, she mastered every detail to ensure her guests were comfortable and content.

Townspeople called her Mother Slough because she provided tender mothering to her patrons. Exhausted travelers, seeking repose in Peoria, happily accepted her invitation to rest and refuel in the establishment of her husband. On the prairie, it was a customary practice for the wife to stay in the background while the husband handled business matters. Anna, allowing Jacob to save face, acted the role of the dutiful wife, seemingly satisfied to handle mundane household activities while Jacob entertained customers with lively conversation and libation. Actually, she was the driving force that kept the business profitable.

As quoted from Bateman's *History of Peoria County:*

> Mr. Slough was blessed with a buxom, good-looking wife of rare executive ability, who gave every detail of the business, out of doors as well as in, her personal supervision, and left "Jakey" as Mr. Slough was familiarly called, but little to do except to entertain guests and attend the bar.

Puffy pillows, clean beds, and well-maintained rooms were hallmarks of the Sloughs' hospitality. German guests were especially attracted there when they heard about Anna's hearty portions of sausages, dumplings, and kraut. Visitors often read of such bed-and-breakfast hotels in special guidebooks written to aid travelers in selecting a particular town or business. The Sloughs' good reputation ensured the business was featured in these pamphlets.

Life was comfortable for the Sloughs. The hotel was flourishing, and life in bustling Peoria suited their personalities. However, Anna didn't have time to rest in satisfaction.

Jacob's sudden foray into politics virtually halted their bar business when, as a new member of the Peoria Temperance Society, he took an active stance against serving liquor. While Jacob spoke at temperance meetings requesting the repeal of the law permitting the sale of liquor, Anna devised another plan to make money.

To Anna, coming up with another business was no greater feat than crossing the Allegheny Mountains by herself five years earlier. Using old family recipes, she created tonics and elixirs to cure the ills of Peoria's residents. She placed advertisements for her remedies in Peoria's *Register and North Western Gazetteer* newspaper, touting her two best sellers: the Celebrated Gilder Cordial and Mrs. Jacob Slough's Vegetable Anti-Bilious Dispeptic Pills.

Anna claimed the cordial healed fever and ague. Ague, which is described as "alternate intervals of chills, fever and sweating," was a common malady that plagued residents of prairie communities. The vegetable anti-bilious dispeptic pills purportedly healed a wide variety of ailments from impurities of the blood to closed pores. Anna's advertising and marketing skills are evidenced by the somewhat biased views provided in frank testimonials "from gentlemen well known in Fulton and Peoria counties." Thomas Bryant of Peoria signed the following advisory:

> I hereby certify I have used Mrs. Slough's Anti-Bilious Pills and having received personal benefit there from, and witnessed their good effects on others, recommend them to the public as an invaluable medicine.

Another gentleman by the name of Benont Haskin of New Farmington concurred with a similar recommendation:

> I hereby certify that I have used a number of boxes of Mrs. Slough's Anti-Bilious Dispeptic Pills, and believe them to be the best medicine I have ever used; and I have also witnessed their good effects on numerous other persons.

In case these testimonials were not convincing enough, Anna advised readers that a "long list of certificates might be given if necessary" for those yet uncertain of the healing powers of the medications. Adult doses were one to five pills, "according to the constitution to be taken on going to bed." The recommended dosage for children was one-forth to one-half of a pill every twenty-four hours.

Anna's medicines kept the family afloat financially until the couple ventured back into hotel keeping. It is unclear what changed Jacob's mind, but on April 17, 1840, the couple opened the Union Hotel on Water Street, near the steamboat landing. Word of mouth and the guarantee of hospitality attracted many exhausted trail travelers. Again, Anna settled into her role as the consummate hostess, offering satisfying meals and airy rooms. It is doubtful that liquor was served in the new location, because Jacob's temperance activities continued for many years beyond the opening of the new business. Liquor aside, as luck would have it, just as the hotel began attracting new clientele, an economic downturn threatened the country.

In 1832, President Andrew Jackson vetoed legislation that would renew the charter of the Second National Bank, carrying out what some have called a "personal vendetta" against the nation's largest lending institution. The move caused panic in the banking industry, resulting in the recall of loans and a scarcity of currency circulating within the general population. Residents removed from the population centers of the East Coast were particularly impacted by the lack of available money.

Land speculators, who had been driving the economy in Illinois, reacted in one of two ways: Either they withdrew their properties from the market to avoid selling too cheaply, or they dumped their holdings to raise quick cash just to cover everyday expenses. Gradually, the wave of hopeful eastern speculators dried up, and by the 1840s, the dwindling number of new settlers and tourists affected the bottom line of virtually every Peoria business, from river travel, to farming, to industry.

The Sloughs pushed on, addressing potential patrons with newspaper advertisements that heralded a room price reduction to "correspond with the hardness of the times." Since the new location featured a stable, they included the care of guests' horses as an extra benefit, promising "hay and grain and a faithful and attentive ostler always in attendance."

Without tenants, there was little the couple could do to keep the hotel afloat. Anna realized that during this national calamity, the hotel business would no longer be a viable way to earn income. In an attempt to divert the family from financial ruin, she convinced Jacob to move to their farmland in nearby Richwoods Township. There they built a house and settled into farming the land, which was a more practical lifestyle for the times.

By now, several of the Slough children were married and starting their own families. Anna made certain they had ample farmland to build their own homes and carve out a living. Sadly, only seven of Anna and Jacob's eleven children survived to take advantage of the land that Anna secured.

The eldest son, Jacob W. Slough Jr., seemed to have inherited his mother's adventurous spirit. He repeatedly traveled to Oregon and California to work in the mines before finally settling in Illinois on a parcel of land his mother had purchased from the government years before.

As an elderly woman, Anna must have relished the fact that she'd accomplished her goal. Her children were the beneficiaries of her ambitious undertaking more than forty-five years earlier, when she had first braved the trip from Pennsylvania to the unknown west of Illinois.

Anna died on August 4, 1878, in her Richwoods Township home, surrounded by the rich prairie farmland she had gallantly claimed in 1832. She is laid to rest in Peoria's Springdale Cemetery. Her spirit of determination exemplifies the dauntlessness of the thousands of women who dared to overcome challenges for the good of their family. She will always own the affectionate title of Mother Slough.

EMMA HALE SMITH

1804–1879

Wife of a Prophet

EMMA STEADIED HERSELF WITH THE FIRST STEP, and then gathered seven-year-old Julia and six-year-old Joseph III close to her before fully venturing onto the rutted ice of the frozen Mississippi River. Once they started the almost mile-long crossing, Emma knew that her oldest children would be on their own, as her arms would be laden with two-year-old Freddy and baby Alex. Her own balance would be challenged by the muslin pockets sewn inside her skirt that held her husband's important documents. This was not the activity that Emma would have selected on that bitter February day in 1839. She and the children were already exhausted, having trekked more than 225 miles across the state of Missouri.

For the Smith family, running for their lives was a way of life. Emma harbored the silent hope that this would be the last time they would be forced to leave their home. All she really wanted was to feel safe and to live peacefully with her family. Little did Emma know that after her husband joined her in Illinois, they would make the tiny town of Commerce their home, and her wish to plant permanent roots there would become a reality.

Joseph Smith, the religious prophet of the Church of Latter-day Saints, and Emma's husband, changed the name of the Illinois town from Commerce to the Hebrew word "Nauvoo," which means "beautiful habitation for man." Every day, the exodus from Missouri spilled hundreds of Mormons into the Nauvoo. Emma found herself ministering to them, managing her children, and tending to chores. She tolerated Joseph's dinner meetings with church members. There was very little time for herself. Emma's modest log house, named the Old Homestead, was immaculate. She worked from morning to night, and no one seems to have recorded that she complained about her station. She loved having a home of her own, and it was especially wonderful to have Joseph there, although life as his wife had been challenging beyond her wildest dreams.

Emma Hale grew up in eastern Pennsylvania along a bend of the rushing Susquehanna River. She was a religious girl raised in the strict Methodist tradition, and she prayed fervently to God when she was a very young child. Scholarly studies escaped her other than reading the scriptures and learning to write, but no one doubted her keen intelligence. Her family farmed and supplemented their income by welcoming boarders into their Harmony, Pennsylvania, home. Thus the tall, brown-eyed, black-haired beauty met the dashing, blue-eyed, blond-haired young man who would become her spouse.

Joseph Smith arrived from New York in search of a home away from home while he worked as a laborer. Smitten by his outspoken religious views, and his obvious interest in her, Emma daringly courted Joseph under the disapproving eyes of her parents. Mr. and Mrs. Hale were so adverse to the match that they vehemently refused Joseph's request for Emma's hand in marriage, citing his lack of a reasonable income to support her. Emma and Joseph had other plans, and ironically, they established a pattern of running away early in their relationship.

EMMA HALE SMITH

According to Emma, she had no intention of marrying Joseph during a clandestine meeting in January 1827. Aware of the gravity of disobeying her parents, Emma accepted Joseph's proposal and they eloped that day. Fear of her parents' anger and disapproval was measured in the fact that, rather than returning home to Harmony, she instead fled to New York, into the home of Joseph's parents. With this break from her family, Emma cleaved to her husband. She would follow him in his spiritual journey with little question.

After moving to New York, Joseph borrowed a neighbor's wagon and called to Emma to join him on a short ride to a place called Hill Cumorah. It's not clear whether or not, on that cool morning, Emma had an inkling of Joseph's plan. When he descended from the hilltop with news of his encounter with an angel, and bearing the physical proof of engraved tablets that he called the "ancient record of gold," Emma relied on her devotion to her husband and her deep faith to resolve the story. Joseph kept the tablets covered and shielded from her eyes, and although she never saw them, she wrote of hearing the metal clinking inside of their wrapper and admitted to touching along the rim of the edge of the books while dusting. She always honored Joseph's request that she not view the tablets. The events of this day would bring both favor and a curse upon her family.

Together the couple set about translating the sacred scriptures. Illuminated by the flickering light of candles, Joseph and Emma sat at the wooden dinner table; Joseph read the sacred writ aloud while Emma transcribed the codex. When news of the holy book spread, Emma found herself in the unenviable position of hiding the writings from would-be thieves. Enraged strangers, intolerant of non-traditional religions, accosted her outside of her home as she hung laundry or tended to her garden. They demanded she divulge Joseph's whereabouts, and show them the writings, but she managed to divert their attention and escape their requests. These early incidents of unexpected visits and stalking foreshadowed the life

Emma would lead during her nearly eighteen-year marriage to the Prophet Joseph Smith.

In December 1837, Emma and Joseph accepted an olive branch of reconciliation from the Hales back in Harmony. The agreement was cordial: The couple would live in a small home on Emma's parents' land, and Joseph would farm a designated area. However, after settling in, Joseph opted instead to concentrate on publishing the holy book and preaching the Gospel according to the Book of Mormon. The fuse was lit and on a slow burn.

Emma's father clashed with them, complaining that Joseph was not living up to his word, not to mention the humiliation caused when Joseph was arrested twice during the two and a half years they lived in the little cabin. This time the bridges were burned. The showdown left Emma facing the sad decision of selecting between her husband and her family; she chose her husband and a life of exile from her home and her parents' affections.

The couple began the journey to Kirkland, Ohio, where many Mormons (Latter-day Saints) were settling. Emma and Joseph were poor, and arrived without anything of real value, so they depended on the charity of others to survive. It was an embarrassing state of affairs for Emma, but she was grateful for the generosity of others, especially since she was expecting her first child.

The Smiths experienced the thrill of becoming parents and the tragedy of death all in one day: Their baby died within hours of birth. An incredible turn of events alleviated their grief when word came that a gentleman in a nearby town had suffered the loss of his wife in childbirth after she delivered healthy twins. Unable to care for the baby boy and girl, he agreed to let the Smiths adopt them. Finally, Emma felt the contentment of motherhood, even though she worried about not having a home in which to rear them.

The Smiths continued to live the life of wanderers. Although they were welcomed into the home of friends in Hiram, Ohio, news of the Prophet's arrival so agitated the townspeople that a mob formed and forced their way upstairs to where the Smith family slept. They dragged Joseph into the street, where he was beaten, tarred, and feathered.

Petrified, Emma swaddled the tiny twins who were recovering from the measles. She was certain she would never see Joseph alive. However, as he had managed so many times before, he escaped with his life and returned to the residence. His injuries so startled Emma that she fainted at the sight of her naked, brutalized husband. Grateful for his return, she worked feverishly throughout the night, using grease to ease the removal of tar from his open wounds. The cycle of fear continued for Emma.

The Smiths eventually traveled to western Missouri to join a large, established Mormon settlement. It wasn't long before Joseph's politics and preaching brought the wrath of Missouri's governor, who handed down a horrific order of Mormon extermination. Abandoning virtually all possessions, including their homes, thousands fled the decree. Emma was among them, as the Mormons braved the crystallized waves of the daunting Mississippi River. Emma managed her children alone as Joseph languished within the walls of a Missouri jail. Although the Smiths were reunited in Illinois, the Prophet's controversial teachings continued to dog them and the church.

Probably the most spectacular curiosity of the early Mormon Church is the discussion of polygamy. There are many diametrically opposed views of what Emma knew or didn't know about the practice. Some speculate that Joseph entered into plural marriage while in Ohio, but it is believed that Emma was unaware of the teachings until early 1843. Ironically, it was Joseph himself who unwittingly placed Emma into the public forum where she could share what some have recorded as her less than supportive views of a wife's "religious duty" to accept the concept of multiple wives, also known as celestial marriage. Had he known the true power of Emma, Joseph probably would have never created the Female Relief Society and appointed her president.

Upon arriving at Nauvoo, Emma was overwhelmed with caring for hundreds of needy souls who had contracted malaria from the mosquitoes flourishing along the town's boggy riverbed. She spearheaded clothing drives and arranged for food and shelter for those just arriving in town from throughout the United States and England. Her charitable acts warranted support, so Joseph instituted the Nauvoo Female Relief Society and Emma was duly elected its president. With this office, Emma was "ordained to teach" the women membership and, to the chagrin of the male church hierarchy who recorded events in their diaries, that's what she did.

When Joseph explained the concept of plural marriage to Emma, she balked. As the obedient wife of the Prophet and a devoted Mormon, she felt compelled to honor her husband and follow the precepts of the Mormon Church. In order to present a proper role model, Emma suppressed her anger under the condition that she be the one to select new wives for Joseph. The decision tortured her soul.

Like a sapling buffeted to and fro during a violent storm, Emma's support of the secret teaching vacillated. Raw moments were punctuated with painful betrayals, such as the discovery that her dearest female friend was also married to Joseph. Emma engaged Joseph in heated arguments that spanned from dusk to dawn. During one confrontation, she boldly threatened divorce, prompting Joseph to pledge that he would abandon the polygamist lifestyle. It is said that Emma believed his claims, yet he maintained marriage relationships with many wives up until his death. For generations, scholars within and outside of the Mormon Church have bandied about various theories regarding how much Emma knew, and whether or not she truly accepted the practice.

Whatever she said in private, she appeared to dismiss it in public by urging all to follow the pulpit teachings of Prophet Smith. However, records indicate that Emma used the podium of the Female Relief Society to plant the subtle, subversive idea that if the Prophet's public teachings were to be honored, his private teachings should be ignored. The more than 1,000 women members of the society understood her message, and Emma's crusade against plural marriage took root. Joseph's diary entries, and the journals of men within his inner circle, collaborate that he was frustrated by Emma's anti-polygamy stance. The men's council moved to have the society disbanded, and it remained so for nearly ten years.

Joseph's political aspirations caused anxiety among the citizenry of Hancock County. Already disturbed by the unusual city charter first extended to Nauvoo a year after the Mormons deemed the place home, the old-time residents witnessed Joseph Smith avoid prosecution, shielded by that clever city charter. Many felt it extended unfair advantage to the Mormons. Additionally, there was tension over the Nauvoo Legion, a city militia boasting more than 1,500 members in 1841 and commanded by Lieutenant-General Joseph Smith. When Smith agreed to run for the office of the president of the United States, it was the last straw for locals and government officials who were wary of an attempted Mormon takeover of the United States. Religion aside, many citizens felt Joseph Smith and his army were a threat to the very fabric of American freedom.

A vigilante group comprised of several hundred men attacked and murdered Joseph and his brother outside of the jail in Carthage, Illinois, on June 27, 1844. Emma finally received the news she had dreaded for years. During the viewing of his body, she expressed her loss by saying, "My husband was my crown; for him and for my children I have suffered the loss of all things."

In the seven years they lived together in Nauvoo, Joseph was arrested, in exile, or traveling for much of the time, while Emma maintained their business ventures and nurtured their children. Joseph had always managed to return home to her. Now he was gone.

Shortly after the funeral, there was speculation that Emma would become a plural wife of the new church leader Brigham Young. Emma flatly rejected the idea. She had never fully agreed to such an arrangement with the man she loved; she would not consider it with a man she did not. Young further perturbed her by asking for Joseph's desk, papers, and other church-related artifacts. Standing up to the powerful church leadership, she refused to relinquish her guardianship of the precious documents entrusted to her by Joseph. Thirty years later, Emma commented, "I still feel a sacredness attached to them."

By fall, the Mormons received notice from the surrounding counties that they would be evicted from Nauvoo if they did not leave on their own accord. Church leaders announced that the Saints would move west. Not everyone agreed with the order.

Emma was on her last nerve. She had been rebuffed by authorities when she traveled to Quincy to demand an inquest into the death of her husband, and she was recovering from the birth of her last child. Understandably, her prime concerns were her now fatherless children and the legacy of her husband. Joseph was buried in Nauvoo and there she would stay. It was a decision that caused bitterness toward Emma, as the Saints felt she had turned her back on the church.

When the first wagons rolled toward Utah in January 1845, Emma stood staunchly by her window. Years later, her snub prompted Brigham Young to write, "I never saw a day in the world that I would not almost worship that woman, Emma Smith, if she would be a saint instead of being a devil."

Emma's plan to remain in Nauvoo was challenged when outsiders continued to threaten invasion and war on the remnant of the community. Within months the new widow was forced to flee from her home with her children in tow. They settled for six months in Fulton, Illinois, until quieter times permitted a safe return to the Nauvoo Mansion House that Emma and Joseph had shared.

After a suitable mourning period, Emma was approached by a local gentleman who proposed marriage. Tongues were set wagging when, on December 23, 1847, Emma became the wife of a non-Mormon named "Major" Lewis C. Bidamon. Emma ignored the idle chatter and resumed a normal home life, free from the terror of the past. She was skilled at making salves and herbal medicines, and when neighbors' children fell ill, the doctor often sent them to Emma for treatment. Every day her superb soprano voice could be heard outside as she sang her daily devotional to God. She also loved riding her favorite steed in the fields. She did not abandon the memory of Joseph; every day she wore the simple golden bead necklace that he'd given her.

As she aged, the community rallied around her with great respect. Children clamored at her door for a cookie, and she always had plenty on hand to spoil each cherubic tot that begged for more. Emma's daily routine included prayer, housework, gardening, and writing lengthy letters. The Major built them a new home, which delighted her. Nearly every day Emma received visitors and chatted freely with those asking about the Mormons. When guests pried, she responded, "Thank you—those things are personal."

The last five years of her life brought a veritable parade of journalists, Saints from Utah, and the curious to her front porch. Some attempted to shame her for not supporting the Mormons' move to Utah. Emma would not be bullied: Such behavior brought a door slammed in the face or a tart response.

On at least three occasions, Emma granted formal interviews to discuss the early Mormon Church. It appears that her answers changed depending on the identity of the interviewer. Sometimes she protected the legacy with responses cloaked in theology. Other times, she adeptly deflected the truth. One interviewer felt Emma tacitly responded "yes" to the question of Joseph Smith's polygamist activities by leaving the room rather than verbalizing the word. As always, her first concern was shielding her children, particularly Joseph III and Alexander, who were active in the leadership of the Reorganized Church, which had spun off from the Mormon Church after Joseph's death. Her behavior just added to the mystery.

Even contemporaries were baffled by her ambiguous and seemingly contradictory replies. Unfortunately, the polygamy question overshadowed Emma's devotion to those she loved, her commitment to healing the sick, and her unwavering dedication toward those in need at her own physical and mental expense.

Emma died on April 30, 1879. She was laid to rest beside her first husband, the Prophet. With her she took the deepest secrets of her life with Joseph Smith. Questions about her loyalty to the Mormon Church, her views on plural marriage, and her relationship with her husband would forever be unanswered. Some called her a traitor, others a champion. Perhaps the truest title would be enigma, and Emma probably would have liked it that way.

LYDIA MOSS BRADLEY

1816–1908

For the Children

A CRISP FALL BREEZE SWIRLED LEAVES ALONG the walkways of Bradley Polytechnic Institute on October 8, 1907, as guests arrived for the tenth anniversary celebration of Founder's Day. Inside Bradley Hall, Mrs. Lydia Moss Bradley, founder and benefactor, sat on stage among faculty members dressed in full regalia.

A petite and fragile-looking woman, the ninety-one-year-old dowager displayed complete composure, and pithy and alert, fully aware of the importance of the day. Her attire was formal, from the fancy decorated hat to the long, black silk dress reminiscent of a bygone era. An ascot of delicate white lace, folded neatly at her neckline, was secured by a funeral brooch bearing the likeness of Tobias, her late husband. It was appropriate that she would honor Tobias on this day, as the school had also been his dream. For Lydia, the school was a tribute to her treasured family.

Lydia's story began on July 31, 1816, in the tiny river town of Vevay in Switzerland County, Indiana. Born in the family farm-house, Lydia was the youngest daughter of Virginia natives Zeally Moss and his second wife, Jenny Glasscock.

As in many river towns, life in Vevay was both modestly cosmopolitan and rural. The settlement extended to the riverbank and became a natural docking point for river traffic. Spring floods often churned the muddy Ohio River into those homes and businesses too close to the edge. This almost yearly ritual of nature created a community where neighbors helped each other in the lean times and smart settlers never let down their guard. Survival depended on hard work and ingenuity. It was this mind-set that helped form the pioneer spirit of the six Moss children.

Little Lydia was the darling of her father. She was a tiny girl but bright in thought. Zeally sometimes spoiled Lydia, surprising her with trinkets purchased from store boats that docked along the river. Once he delighted her with a small bowl adorned with a colorful painted peacock. It was a treasure that she kept for her entire life.

Despite the seeming favoritism, Lydia was expected to contribute to the family. She joined her mother and sisters in the prairie woman's household arts of churning butter, growing and canning vegetables, baking bread, putting up lard, smoking meats, and cooking fine meals. There were times spent sewing and spinning and tending to household and farm chores.

School for Lydia was spent within the chinked and daubed walls of the rustic log cabin home of schoolmarm Mrs. Campbell. Books were precious and few, and lessons were taught using the Bible and the English Reader. Students were responsible for making their own quill writing instruments and inks. Although she was eager to learn, Lydia admitted that she wasn't always a model student. Mrs. Campbell disciplined Lydia by having her stand in the corner with a ruler in her mouth. The primitive education Lydia received in front of the crackling fire was suitable for life in a farm town. From her father Zeally, she learned a common-sense approach to solving problems.

When it came to supporting his family, Zeally Moss wore many hats. As a Revolutionary War captain and quartermaster, he had acquired business skills that he adapted into successful civilian enterprises. He also served as a Baptist minister and enjoyed his role as a gentleman farmer. Of all of his ventures, Zeally was particularly adept at buying and selling land. As his children grew and moved away to begin their own lives, Zeally generously granted acreage to each of them. Through his example, Lydia understood the value of owning land.

In the mid-1830s, when Lydia was a teenager, Zeally presented her with a foal. Lydia raised the animal with care, turning it into a fine saddle horse that gave her both freedom and transportation. However, when the budding entrepreneur discovered an opportunity to trade the horse for a wooded parcel, she did so, realizing that, unlike the land, the horse was no longer appreciating in value. Delighted by her foresight, Zeally did not stop his daughter's foray into real estate. Lydia was quite proud of her property, and she carefully calculated the proceeds expected from harvesting the wood and farming.

Despite her small stature, Lydia cleared the underbrush and trees herself. When she accumulated a reasonable stack, she hauled the timbers to the local sawmill to sell. Her determination and, perhaps, her long dark hair and fine looks must have impressed the hardworking young mill owner. His name was Tobias Smith Bradley.

Tobias was five years her senior, but he and Lydia shared many things in common. Tobias also came from Revolutionary War stock and his family hailed from Virginia. The die for a marriage was cast.

After a courtship, Tobias and Lydia married on May 11, 1837. True to her work ethic, Lydia made the wedding clothes for both herself and her groom. They settled on the Bradley homestead at Log Lick near Vevay. The industrious Lydia took in boarders when money was tight, making her days long and chores unending.

When Vevay's economy hit hard times, the Bradleys discussed moving to start anew. Tobias suggested relocating to Kentucky, where his father had served in the state legislature. Lydia bristled at the prospect of living in a slave state.

Lydia's brother, Captain William Moss, proposed they join him in the growing Illinois River town of Peoria. Although Peoria boasted a population of nearly 4,000, it was not unlike Vevay in that it thrived on riverboat trade. There was plenty of available land, plus Captain Moss offered Tobias a job. The scenario seemed ideal.

Lydia sold the Indiana parcel she had acquired as a young woman with the trade of her horse, as well as her ownership in a farm given to her by her father. Between the sale of the land and her dowry, Lydia amassed $7,000 for the trip to Peoria.

She and her husband purchased a large tract on Peoria's perimeter and set up housekeeping with their four-year-old daughter, Clarissa, and Lydia's mother, Jenny. Having family already in Peoria eased the transition, plus Lydia's father, who had died while visiting Captain Moss in 1839, was buried nearby, and it comforted Lydia and her mother to be close to his grave.

Initially, life in Peoria was exciting. Lydia settled into domestic happiness, giving birth to a son shortly after their arrival. Caring for the children and maintaining the house were just part of her daily routine. Lydia, not entirely relinquishing business matters to her husband, actively participated in managing the money secured from renting their farmland.

Tobias partnered with his brother-in-law in a wide variety of business ventures, including distilleries, steamboats, and flour and saw mills, the Peoria Pottery Company, real estate, railroad investment, and banking. Just as the couple's financial wealth and social status emerged, unspeakable tragedy beset their most precious gifts—their children.

All of the Bradleys' affluence could not protect their family from the deadly childhood illnesses that stalked youngsters of that era. Pioneers on the prairie and city folk alike suffered greatly from the lack of adequate medicines and medical treatment. One by one the Bradley children succumbed: Clarissa, age four; Tobias Jr., age seven months; Mary, age ten months; William, age two. Rebecca, age six, had died before the Bradleys relocated to Peoria. There were sad coincidences in their deaths. William died ten years to the day after their first child Rebecca died. Mary died exactly ten months after her birth. Tobias Jr. and Clarissa passed sixteen days apart just before Christmas in 1847. It was the first Christmas that Lydia and Tobias celebrated in Peoria, and they celebrated it alone.

On April 24, 1849, a new baby girl buoyed the Bradley household. They named her Laura, and she grew into a thin child with delicate facial features that favored her mother. Photographs show her with dark, shoulder-length hair arranged in perfectly formed finger curls. Laura was understandably the focus of her parents' devotion. Friends who visited the Bradley home noticed that Laura returned their affection by sitting on her parents' laps and hugging them without reserve.

Lydia sent Laura to public school and gave her a new piano and private lessons. Laura wore fashionable clothing and a gold pendant around her neck. Mother and daughter were especially close. Knowing her mother's love for beautiful china, Laura surprised Lydia with a hand-painted cup and saucer that featured a blue moss design. Lydia cherished the present. It was one of the last gifts enjoyed between the two.

On February 3, 1864, the unthinkable happened again. Fourteen-year-old Laura fell ill and died suddenly. Reeling from the loss, the Bradleys made no public statements. Instead, their feelings were displayed at dinner each night as Lydia's best china, silverware, and crystal drinking glass sat unused at Laura's place. Lydia and Tobias sat mute. It was as if they fully expected their cherubic teenager to reappear in her dining room chair, late from her piano lesson or delayed by friends. As their silverware clinked against their plates, the silence of Laura's absent voice was deafening. Meals were lonely for the Bradleys, even with company present. A close friend noted that over many years, only once did Lydia mention one of her children during a private conversation.

Realizing they were of the age at which there would be no more children, Lydia and Tobias contemplated opening an orphanage. Plans were moving forward when, before the end of 1867, fate would again intervene.

As he always did before buying land, Tobias set out to investigate a potential acquisition located on the other side of the Illinois River. Lydia remained home, tending to her self-assigned tasks. Toward evening someone pounded on her door. Tobias had been found, dazed and bleeding along the side of a road after his carriage had collapsed. He was carried to a distant home to rest overnight, leaving Lydia to agonize over his return. Before dawn she stood sentry on the front porch, praying for a miracle as the wagon carrying Tobias approached.

At first, Tobias rallied at hearing her voice. He answered simple questions when she cooled his head with a damp cloth, and he attempted to focus on her face as she smiled down on him. For all of her attention, devotion, and love, however, there was nothing that could be done. Any glimmer of hope that Lydia held for his recovery was dashed when he lost consciousness. Just seven days before their thirtieth wedding anniversary, Tobias died.

Lydia had lost six children and now her husband. Still, she went into her garden and tended to her roses, worked in the kitchen, and collected eggs from one of her farms. When the day came to bury Tobias, she donned her finest black dress and joined the mourners who gathered in Peoria from throughout the country. In the custom of the day, Lydia placed a mourning brooch at her neck. The gold case bore his image and contained a lock of Tobias's hair. Lydia wore the pin every day, and for the rest of her life it would remain an external token of her internal grief.

Showing their great respect for her business acumen, the Board of Directors of the First National Bank of Peoria asked Lydia to take her husband's position, making her the first woman in the nation to be named the president of a bank. Lydia stepped into her husband's role and expanded her daily tasks to include managing his accounts. She was known to finish a full day of appointments and chores and then pull on work boots to meet a surveyor in a muddy field. One issue consumed Lydia—the construction of an orphanage. There was a hitch, however; Tobias had not registered a written will.

It was an oversight that froze Lydia's survivor benefits and jeopardized her plans for years. By the time the courts awarded her Tobias's $500,000 estate, Lydia had changed course, realizing that young people would benefit more from learning a trade.

Lydia hired respected Peoria lawyer W. W. Hammond to advise her. Every morning for twenty-two years, until Lydia's death, Hammond arrived at her home with a briefcase full of papers. The pair sat in the front parlor at the black walnut breakfast table and Lydia learned how to become a hands-on manager. She read every document, reviewed all transactions, discussed new business, signed checks, and processed receipts from her properties. Over several years, Lydia grew her fortune from $500,000 to $1 million. She also owned real estate and various businesses.

The Peoria Watch Company was a Bradley enterprise, and in 1892 Lydia acquired controlling interest in Parson's Horological School of LaPorte, Indiana. Parson's was America's first school chartered to educate watchmakers, and it met Lydia's criteria of an academy that would teach a trade. She relocated Parson's and associated it with the already established Peoria watch repair business. It was a start, but not exactly the scope of what she envisioned.

During this time, higher education in Illinois was changing to include what would become the first junior college system in the nation. The concept was the brainchild of the University of Chicago's president, Dr. William Rainey Harper, and the idea paralleled Lydia's; students would graduate with trade experience. Lydia thought that, because of finances, her school would be built after her death. Dr. Harper offered a solution.

The creation of a life estate would allow Lydia to fund a school while she was alive and give her the power to make decisions and direct construction of the institution. Lydia loved to control details, so the proposal was very appealing.

With Harper's guidance, Bradley Polytechnic Institute was chartered on November 13, 1896. At age eighty, Lydia headed the charge to secure architectural drawings, employ contractors, hire teachers, establish a curriculum, and enroll students for an October 1897 dedication. Critics said it couldn't be done. Lydia's pioneer spirit didn't let her down.

The dedication ceremony, which later became Founder's Day, was held on October 8, 1897, as Lydia had planned, and culminated with the simple gesture of her handing the keys for the buildings to the president of the school's Board of Trustees. Three months later, Lydia paid off the mortgages owed on all of the institute's buildings.

Lydia relished seeing the students on campus and, until her age caught up with her, she accepted invitations to various school programs. Young people energized her.

She rarely complained about her health, despite persistent bouts with cystitis. On December 27, 1907, Dr. A. L. Corcoran was summoned to Lydia's rosewood bedstead. Weak but alert, Lydia complained of a sore throat and the grippe. She appeared frail, but her mind was clear and decisive and she refused all pain medication. Lydia told her nurse that she hoped to be buried on a day filled with sunshine. It was one of her last conversations.

Lydia Moss Bradley died peacefully in the early morning of January 16, 1908. As would be expected of this organized woman, she left nothing to chance regarding her funeral, having crafted the details in her own handwritten instructions.

Peoria recognized its benefactor by lowering its flags to half-mast, an honor that it had never before bestowed upon a female citizen. Lydia had been a good steward to the city. She had donated land for the Laura Bradley Park, a hospital, and homes for aged women and for orphans, and she was instrumental in creating Peoria's Park District.

As the cortege passed through Peoria, a singular bell tolled one strike for each year of her life. She was buried on a bitterly cold winter day, with winds howling and yet, in contrast, the sun was shining brightly, causing the frozen snow to glitter along the route. It was sunny, just as she'd hoped.

Upon her death, long-lost relatives hotly contested her will, hoping for a piece of the financial pie. Lydia had more than 130 known relatives, mostly the children and grandchildren of her brothers and sisters. Attorneys accused W. W. Hammond and her housekeeper of altering the document without Lydia's consent.

Another challenger claimed Lydia was mentally unstable and pointed to her use of clairvoyants to contact departed loved ones as evidence. One series of seemingly supernatural events ended with Lydia being defrauded by a greedy huckster maid who staged bizarre encounters to convince Lydia that Tobias and Laura were leaving her gifts and moving furniture. While Lydia preoccupied herself with the fantastic goings-on, the maid helped herself to Lydia's keys and the weekly rent money that Lydia had locked away in her bureau drawers. Embarrassingly, this ghost story made its way into the pages of the *New York Times!*

Rumors circulated that Lydia kept secrets. As a woman of wealth, Lydia coveted her privacy, and those around her protected her interests. Proof of that lay in the fact that her obituary revealed she had remarried and divorced after Tobias's death. Her second husband was southern businessman Edward E. Clark. The marriage was brief and Lydia was ahead of her time, having insisted on executing a prenuptial agreement. The wording was clear: In case of divorce or death, each would leave the marriage without the financial advantage of the other.

The courts upheld her will, which bequeathed all but $10,000 of her $2.8 million fortune to the school; her estate and property would remain in the hands of Bradley Polytechnic Institute. On a personal note, Lydia's will provided for all descendants of her father, Zeally Moss, to receive free tuition at Bradley. She also stipulated that flowers and Christmas wreaths be laid yearly on the graves of her family.

Lydia was a dichotomy—generous yet frugal; daring yet conservative; old-fashioned yet modern; reclusive yet engaged in public enterprises. Here was a woman who churned butter during business meetings, yet served tea to guests from her gold-banded tea set. Her home was large, but much of the furniture was inherited from family members. Her dining room featured hand-painted wall decorations and expensive cut-glass vases, yet the table was filled with food planted and harvested by her own hands. Few words of Lydia's remain in any source other than hearsay, as her personal papers were lost or destroyed upon her death.

In 1920, the school became a four-year institution, and in 1946 it was renamed Bradley University. Today, a life-size bronze statue of the elegantly dressed Mrs. Lydia Moss Bradley stands in the commons, where students pass by on their way to classes. Through her benefaction, thousands of men and women have received degrees and contributed to the welfare and betterment of their families and communities, just as Lydia intended. True to her legacy and purpose, Lydia's bittersweet words are displayed on campus for all to read:

DEDICATED TO THE MEMORY OF MY BELOVED HUSBAND
TOBIAS S. BRADLEY AND OUR DECEASED CHILDREN, BY LYDIA BRADLEY.

CANDACE McCORMICK REED

1818–1900

Prairie Portraits

PLUMES OF BLACK SMOKE ROLLED SILENTLY through the hallway and down the staircase of the commercial building at 403½ Hampshire Street. Undetected, the smoldering fire, which had started in the upper-level photography studio of Mrs. Warren A. Reed, quietly consumed a lifetime of work while the citizens of Quincy slept. Time ticked by before someone unleashed the alarm bell, alerting Quincy's firemen of the emergency.

When she heard the news, sixty-year-old Candace McCormick Reed was fully aware that the insurance had lapsed on the building. She would have to start over from scratch. Without hesitation, she vowed to rebuild the business that had sustained her family.

A true southerner by birth, Candace McCormick gasped her first breath on June 17, 1818, in the hamlet of Crab Orchard, Tennessee. When just a toddler, her parents moved to Canton, Missouri. At age twenty-four, she married a gentleman by the name of Warren A. Reed.

Warren was a photographer at a time when Americans were just beginning their love affair with the fledgling industry. Invented

CANDACE McCORMICK REED

in 1839, the process of photographing an image and creating a daguerreotype was somewhat complicated and time-consuming. The photographer was like a chemist, skilled in the use of copper, silver, iodine vapors, hot mercury, sodium thiosulfate, and gold chloride. Training was necessary to ensure the safety of the operator and the quality of the product.

Shortly after their wedding, Candace began assisting in the business, becoming a skilled apprentice under the tutelage of her husband. She practiced operating the cameras and applying the chemicals and mastered the trade as a touch-up artist. Candace was in a unique position, as women of the era were not typically privy to such a career opportunity.

At the same time, she maintained her home and suffered through the bittersweet reality of early 1800s motherhood, giving birth to three children, of whom only one, a son, survived.

In 1848, the couple bundled up their young son and relocated from Missouri. Traveling some 25 miles, which included crossing the churning currents of the Mississippi River, they settled in Quincy, Illinois. It was a fresh start in a growing town.

Quincy's location on the bank of the Mississippi River made it a magnet for settlers. The Reeds' timing served them well, as the burgeoning city of nearly 6,000 souls was devoid of such a business. The Reeds' studio became the first, and eventually, the oldest photographic shop in town, remaining in business over the next fifty years.

In short order, Warren advertised himself and his wife as "artists" capable of producing portraits "in any weather." Within a few months of their arrival, the Reeds celebrated the birth of another son. The pair volunteered in the community and Warren served as the superintendent of schools from 1852 to 1854. They developed friendships with Quincy's most prominent citizens, including its founder and later the governor of Illinois, John Wood.

The relatively secure Quincy economy helped boost the Reeds' business into one of esteemed success, requiring they move their gallery to a larger location. By the late 1850s, Quincy boasted a population of over 20,000 and there seemed to be no wavering in the city's expansion.

Warren took advantage of this steady marketplace, always searching for a hook to entice customers. McEvoy and Beatty's 1857 *Official Business Directory* listed W. A. Reed and Company as a business that "produced daguerreotypes, ambrotypes and melainotypes on short notice."

The husband–wife team constantly adjusted to the rapid changes in the photography industry by acquiring new cameras and refining methods of production. Their hard work, advertising, community activism, and friendships paid off. They purchased a comfortable home at 709 Broadway Street.

In 1957, the Reeds accepted a plum assignment—the photographic record of the construction of then Illinois Lieutenant Governor John Wood's octagonal home. The contract required that exterior photographs be taken regularly to record the evolution of the construction progress on the unusual, white marble building. The project would span years. Undoubtedly, Warren signed the contract with John Wood. Unexpectedly, it would be Candace who would complete the job.

Thirty-six-year-old Warren died suddenly in 1858, leaving Candace a grieving widow faced with supporting two boys and her elderly mother-in-law. For most women, this would have meant certain poverty. Candace's prospects were much different, however, since she had honed a skill for more than a decade while working side by side with her husband.

Candace attacked the problem with methodical logic. Money was her first concern, so she immediately sold her husband's enterprise in order to raise cash for everyday living expenses. However, she did not abandon the photography business. She realized that it was the best way for her to earn a good living.

Within six months of Warren's untimely death, Candace rented space down the street from the former Reed location and unveiled her new venture in an 1858 newspaper advertisement. She named her daguerreotype shop "The Excelsior Picture Gallery."

Perhaps Candace experienced some reservation that townsfolk might disapprove of her bold independence. She buffered any sense of impropriety by adding a less threatening, more womanly trade at the bottom of one advertisement: "Plain sewing and stitching services are also offered by Mrs. Reed."

Smartly, Candace employed her younger sister Celina as an apprentice and, eventually, as an operator. Drawing from Warren's marketing techniques, Candace ran an advertisement on June 18, 1859, in the *Daily Whig Republican*. The tone was polite and ended with a classic sales line:

Ambrotypes for 50 cents, Mrs. W. A. Reed is now taking very nice Ambrotypes for the above sum for a short time only.

Locals responded to her limited-time offer. Candace demonstrated her eye for design, staging subjects in front of a pedestal, chair, or settee. She incorporated backdrops, draperies, large urns, and vases to enhance visual interest. When a bride and groom posed before the lens, a wedding veil was on hand to perch atop the head of the new wife. Sometimes a floral arrangement or a bouquet prop was provided from Candace's full-service studio.

While honoring the contract to record the construction of Governor Wood's mansion, Candace also photographed buildings along Quincy's streets, turning both projects into a series of stereoscopic views for purchase by the general public.

By 1860, Candace aggressively placed advertisements in local papers as often as three times a week. In the *Daily Whig Republican,* sandwiched in between classifieds for "Hog Feeders" and enrollment dates for Quincy College students, Candace heralded her services, again offering daguerreotypes for the bargain price of 50 cents. Several ads bluntly stated that "Mrs. W. A. Reed's is the place to get your money's worth!" The text continued:

> You can get a nice likeness of yourself or friend, at No. 103 Hampshire Street, over Doway and Morton's Drug Store. Don't forget to wear your dark clothes.

Candace didn't depend solely on Quincy for income. Existing photographs provide evidence that she maintained franchises in two Missouri locations. In 1860, she was listed as the proprietor of a daguerreotype shop in Canton, Missouri, where her brother Wales McCormick lived and worked as a photographer. There are also photographs bearing her insignia that were produced at a branch studio located about 13 miles from Canton in LaGrange, Missouri. This foresight provided a financial buffer for Candace in the months before the war that would change the nation forever.

Quincy was a political hotbed. On October 13, 1858, just weeks after opening her shop, Abraham Lincoln and Stephen A. Douglas debated their views on slavery in Quincy's Washington Park.

Rumors of the impending war gave Candace pause and she moved her Quincy studio into more affordable quarters. The first shots on Fort Sumter in Charleston Harbor, South Carolina, rattled nerves on April 12, 1861. As a concerned businesswoman and mother, Candace ran an urgent reminder of her plight in the April 16th *Daily Whig Republican:*

Excelsior Pictures!!
At the
New Rooms, near the cor. Fourth
And Hampshire Streets.

Mrs. Reed, assisted by Miss McCormack [McCormick], the most experienced operator in this city, has removed to No. 81 Hampshire St., north side of the Public Square, where, with the BEST LIGHT IN TOWN, New Stock, and perfect Cameras, she is prepared to surpass everything in the line of her art.

Pictures in every style of the Photographic art, of all sizes, and at prices to satisfy everybody.

CHILDREN'S PICTURES made quicker and better than ever before. "Patronize the widow, and thus give bread and education to the orphan."

Even with the anxiety of the war in the back of her mind, Candace was full of patriotism. She helped found the Sisters of the Good Samaritan, a social aid society intended to support soldiers and their families. Members accepted financial donations, collected and rolled fabric for bandages, held food drives, and sorted clothing and medicine to be sent to the battlefield. Candace became entrenched in the war effort, leading her to an extraordinary decision.

She convinced her brother to move to Quincy and, with her business in the capable hands of her brother and sister, Candace prepared to don the apron of mercy worn by Civil War nurses.

Prior to her deployment, Candace, Wade, and Celina photographed many individual soldiers. Family images, with men dressed in full military regalia, were poignant keepsakes. A "Cartes de Visite" of a wife or children gained popularity as they were pocket-sized, just 2⅜ inches wide by 4 inches long and, therefore, suitable for a soldier to carry during the long trek into battle.

The 900 soldiers of the Seventy-third Illinois U.S. Infantry Division, along with a modest nursing corps, departed from Quincy in August 1862. An estimated 3,000 to 8,000 women served as Civil War nurses, and Candace was like most, untrained except for homemade remedies. Candace was more skilled with a camera than in the art of nursing, although both tasks were challenging in the face of war.

Photographic equipment of the era lacked the mechanics needed for journalistic photography. The shutter on an 1860s camera was not conducive to snapping rapid-action photographs. Battlefield photographers worked in teams of two, setting up a camera on a tripod so soldiers might pose for one last image. Before and after a battle, photographers meandered around the site, recording scenes for posterity. Despite her potential to be a female battlefield photographer, Candace did not see that as her mission.

During the campaign, many soldiers died from disability and disease. Candace unflinchingly comforted them during their last hours. She knew their mothers, wives, and sweethearts waiting back home. One of the battles fought by the regiment was near Crab Orchard, Tennessee, the birthplace that Candace hadn't seen since she was a child in her mother's arms.

The regiment traveled more than 480 miles from Quincy, and on December 31, 1862, they became entwined in one of the Civil War's most deadly encounters. The North referred to it as the Battle of Murfreesboro after the nearby town. The South called it the Battle of Stones River, after the geographic features of the land. The 4,000-acre parcel turned into a raging storm between the Confederate Army of General Bragg and the troops of Union General Rosecrans. In three days, nearly 25,000 men perished.

Typically, nurses waited at a nearby makeshift hospital. Historians say that few nurses, including notable crusader Clara Barton, entered the theater of battle. Candace broke the rules. It was reported that at the Battle of Murfreesboro, she became one of the first northern women to daringly enter the battlefield.

With gunpowder clouds still fogging the air, she dashed into the sea of injured and dying soldiers, providing immediate triage to suffering victims. Bothered by the brutality of available medical treatment, Candace did exactly what doctors in the field hated: She interceded for those who were facing amputation, arguing with physicians to employ restraint rather than rush to the operating room.

One soldier in particular owed his hand to Candace's negotiations. Captain Henry A. Castle of Quincy suffered an injury that could be quickly resolved with amputation. Candace convinced the attending doctor to permit her to care for Captain Castle's wounds. Once recovery was certain, she served as a hospital transport nurse, accompanying him to New Orleans so he could catch a riverboat back home.

For a year, Candace served in hospitals in Nashville, Vicksburg, and Chattanooga. She spent her own money to purchase necessities for the troops. During trips back to Quincy, she gathered goods and took the responsibility of personally overseeing the delivery of supplies to hometown soldiers. Her actions gained her great respect and affection from the folks at home.

At the end of the war, hometown soldiers marched through the streets of Quincy to rousing cheers. Upon seeing Candace in the crowd, many teary-eyed men broke rank to greet her with a kiss on her gloved hand.

With the war behind her, Candace returned to her flourishing gallery, which, under the management of Celina and Wales, had survived handsomely during her absence. As years passed, there were changes in her business as reflected in the identifying backmark that appeared on the reverse side of her images.

Early after Warren died, her logo was a simple rectangle containing the words "Mrs. W. A. Reed." The next generation of her imprint resembled a scrolled business card surrounded by elegant roses, daffodils, and ferns, with the words "Mrs. W. A. Reed's Art Studio, Quincy, Ill."

By the early 1870s, the back of Candace's photographs displayed an elaborate ink drawing of a ribbon-like banner bearing the inscription, "Mrs. W. A. Reed Quincy, Illinois. Artist." This particular design contained the monogrammed symbol of the prestigious National Photographic Association, a hallmark of distinction awarded to professional photographers.

There was another phrase on the back of most of her photographs: "negatives preserved." It was a promise thwarted on November 28, 1878, when fire ignited the dressing room of her gallery. The studio was a complete loss, including all of the photographs and glass-plate negatives used to produce duplicates.

It is possible that soot-blackened glass negatives could have been salvaged, since the images were imprinted into the glass. Most likely, however, they were discarded as trash along with the remnants of the studio's backdrops, furniture, and fixtures. Candace was faced with rebuilding her livelihood without benefit of insurance. There was no doubt this woman of determination would do just that.

Within the year, the Reed Gallery was back in business, refitted with new cameras, draperies, and accessories. Customers returned for portrait sittings, and, although her patrons were loyal, by the 1880s, the popularity of photography was creating competition.

In 1887, there were seven photographers located just on Hampshire Street alone. Copying her advertising, new businesses offered cut-rate prices and appointments on short notice. One touted that his shop was "built at the rear of the store" so there would be "no going up stairs" for his clients. The pitch was a direct snipe at Candace's third-floor studio, a location she preferred because skylights installed in the ceiling provided the natural light photographers desired for clear, crisp photographs.

Nonetheless, independent newspaper articles recommended Candace's shop, saying, "Mrs. Reed takes photographs and all know that she does it well. If you doubt it, give her a call and see some specimens of her skill."

With the studio thriving again, Candace retired from taking photographs. She earned income by supplying cameras and equipment to several photographers and continued to franchise her good name and reputation for a fee. She rented studio space to her sister Celina and also to a former competitor who specialized in landscape photography.

At the advanced age of eighty-two, Candace suffered what physicians at the time called "a bout of apoplexy." Today it is known as a stroke. After ten days of lapses and rallies, she collapsed in her bed "when the summons came" on April 7, 1900. She rests at Quincy's Woodland Cemetery.

Obituaries commended her for living "a noble life" in which she patriotically supported soldiers and their widows. The *Quincy Daily Whig* stated, "As an American, she should live on the indelible pages of the country's history. In the Civil War, her services will remain a monument to her name."

The *Quincy Daily Herald* called her "one of the most revered residents of the city," continuing, "Her untiring devotion to others and her numberless charitable acts have made her name glorious."

In death, her peers honored her philanthropy and service to Civil War soldiers, and yet, Candace McCormick Reed's name does not command the recognition received by many of the nurses who served alongside her. It's also surprising that, despite being one of the first female photographers in the nation, the novelty of her contribution is generally unknown.

Photographs by Mrs. W. A. Reed currently remain protected in historical societies and private collections. Her artistry provides a glimpse into 1800s America: portraits of early settlers; a stoic bride and groom; the courageous gazes of young soldiers; street scenes of fine brick buildings; a pugilist with hands poised to land a hard right hook; the blurry smile of a squirming infant unable to hold steady while the slow shutter of an ancient camera creates its imprint.

All bear the backmark of a woman photographer who lived in a remarkable time, worked in an uncommon profession, and preserved a photographic legacy for future generations.

MARY TODD LINCOLN

1818–1882

Misunderstood First Lady

WHEN THE CRIPPLED, ELDERLY WOMAN STEPPED gingerly from the carriage, there was no parade, nor were there cheering crowds to greet her. In fact, the day was most unlike the one some twenty years before, when the townspeople of Springfield, Illinois, had waved a fond farewell to their favorite son and her husband, President-Elect Abraham Lincoln. At the time of Lincoln's send-off to Washington on February 11, 1861, Mary was a younger, robust woman, the mother of four cherished boys, and a dedicated wife. There was no inkling then of the tragedies that would horribly scar her mind and heart. Now, the aged Mary lived in a world of memories, of ultimate highs and crushing losses, all imposed upon the backdrop of the tumultuous Civil War. Throughout her public life, the relentless press was rarely her friend, oftentimes publishing hearsay tales of her unstable personality and financial recklessness. The reports overshadowed her accomplishments and generosity, tarnishing her image beyond life.

Mary Jane Todd was born on December 13, 1818, in Lexington, Kentucky, into old-money society. Family described her as

MARY TODD LINCOLN

"high spirited," a personality trait that never tamed with age. Underneath this bright light, six-year-old Mary carried a deep hurt caused by the death of her mother. Reared as a Presbyterian, she had absorbed its lessons of predestination and found comfort in the promise that life continued in glory within heaven's gates.

Her father remarried, but Mary refused to bond with her domineering stepmother. Instead, she clung to her Grandmother Parker, who coddled her with affection, money, and clothes. She also learned to confide in Mammy Sally and many of her father's other fourteen slaves.

Boarding school provided a welcome refuge where Mary escaped into theater, poetry, classic literature, and French. Her Parisian accent was commended as flawless. Most importantly, Mary gained a confidence that gave her the courage to speak her mind.

At home, Mary brazenly invited herself into her father's smoking parlor, where he and his cronies discussed politics and current events. Her quick wit and outspoken views amused the gentlemen. Unbeknownst at the time, these sessions served as grooming for her future role as the wife of a president.

When barely out of her teens, Mary moved to Springfield, Illinois, to live within the handsome brick Italianate home of her sister Elizabeth and brother-in-law, Ninian Edwards. Mary circled within Springfield's dynamic social scene, merrily attracting notable beaux, including the future U.S. Senator Stephen Douglas. Of all the potential suitors, only one, a fellow Kentucky-born gent, caught her eye.

Lanky and somewhat awkward, Abraham Lincoln quickly became smitten by Mary's sparkling blue eyes and her flirtatious flitting of her hand fan. The pairing seemed unconventional to Mary's family. They felt the struggling lawyer was beneath her and told her as much. Mary was keenly aware of his poverty. And it wasn't his looks or charm that drew her to him. He was 6 feet 4 inches tall, careless in dress, and stilted in the finer graces. Mary herself lacked classical physical beauty, but she enhanced her radiant 5-foot-2-inch frame with the latest styles, down to matching gloves and parasol. As her social status dictated, her manners were impeccable. Outward appearances aside, theirs was a deeper attraction.

Both loved reciting poetry, and, like her father, Lincoln enjoyed bantering with Mary on the unwomanly topic of politics. He was the only person who could rival her own ambition, and she loved that about him. So confident was she of his destiny that she boldly announced to a friend that he would be president one day.

Lincoln proposed marriage, and Mary eagerly accepted, but a case of cold feet on the part of her future spouse delayed the wedding for nearly two years. Finally, on a rain-soaked day in November 1842, Mary Todd and Abraham Lincoln stood in the Edwards' parlor and pledged themselves in wedlock. Lincoln placed a golden band on the finger of his wife. The ring was engraved with the testament "Love is Eternal."

While Lincoln traveled for months on the law circuit, Mary settled into domesticity, creating a modest but comfortable home that reflected the proper image for an up-and-coming lawyer. Prior to her marriage, Mary had been the life of the party, surrounded by interesting people and engaged in lively conversations with friends. As a bride she became isolated, withdrawn, and lonely, craving the absent companionship and attention of her husband. She suffered Lincoln's long absences so intensely that she took to her bed for weeks and wrote to him of her blinding headaches and a myriad of other illnesses and uncommon fears. Even thunderstorms caused her so much anxiety that she was moved to tears.

Motherhood provided her with her sole source of constant happy distraction. Robert came first, and Edward followed. Mary also encouraged her husband to follow her father's path into politics and spent much time writing spirited letters of introduction to partisans on his behalf.

When Lincoln won a seat in the United States Congress, Mary shocked many by moving her boys into the crowded Washington boarding house with her husband. Washington society was unimpressed by the freshman Lincolns. Feeling snubbed, Mary took the boys to visit relatives in Kentucky before settling back in Springfield to await the end of Lincoln's two-year term.

For the next several years the couple concentrated on home life and establishing Lincoln's law practice. The year 1850 began with the tragic death of their young son Eddie and ended with the thrill of the birth of William. In 1853 baby Thomas completed the family.

The Lincolns ended their political hiatus in 1854 with a failed senatorial campaign. Despite the defeat, the candidates' debates defined Lincoln's views on slavery, and he became the beacon that drew the eyes of America toward Illinois. Mary actively lobbied, gave interviews and speeches, and entertained key politicians in the lovely parlor of the Lincolns' newly renovated two-story yellow-brown clapboard residence at South Eighth and Jackson Streets. Her prediction of Lincoln's political conquests came true in 1860. His election to the nation's highest office thrust Mary into the spotlight that she very much desired, but for which she was completely unprepared.

During a pre-inaugural trip east, Mary discovered that her elevated status commanded perks that included large amounts of credit at any store of her choice. She splurged on an expensive wardrobe, hoping to impress Washington society. Preoccupied with her celebrity, the American press quickly discovered the sport of trapping naive Mary into sharing her colorful, somewhat negative opinions of Lincoln's potential cabinet members. Her controversial quotes became grist for blistering headlines and caused hard feelings and embarrassment that preceded the president-elect's arrival in Washington.

After the inauguration, the *London Times* referred to Mary as the "First Lady," and thus she became the first presidential wife to be known by the title. In contrast, American editors took jabs by calling her "Our Fair Republican Queen" and "Mrs. President Lincoln."

At the start of the Civil War, President Lincoln was besieged with death threats. He struggled to protect Mary from the rumors, but she must have sensed the danger as civilian patrols stood guard on the White House grounds beneath her windows. Lincoln suggested that Mary flee the drum cadences of soldiers drilling outside the White House portico by taking another trip north. The idea suited her dream of sprucing up the presidential home. The White House was a ramshackle mess, so she requested funds for renovations and repairs. Congress complied by appropriating $20,000, and Mary headed north to the best stores in Philadelphia, New York, and Boston.

Oblivious to budgets, Mary selected an extraordinary array of accoutrements for the national home, quickly surpassing her allotment. Trailing reporters discussed her purchases with unwitting clerks, who verified quantities and disclosed the total charges incurred. The press heralded the details of Mary's financial indiscretion in morning newspapers and exposed her shocking excesses to a nation sacrificing her sons to war.

Ironically, to ease the stress, Mary continued to calm her anxiety with the chime of the cash register. Years later, Mary's sympathetic sister Elizabeth wrote, "It has always been a prominent trait in her character to accumulate a large amount of clothing, and now that she has the means, it seems to be the only available pleasure."

In the midst of war, the tabloid press endlessly picked at Mary's merits and flaws, and there was continual innuendo surrounding her southern roots. The President appeared unscathed, despite sharing the same state of birth as his wife; northerners suspected her of treason, while Confederates branded her a traitor.

The news maintained an unmerciful bias, but she also blundered with seemingly insensitive decisions. At a time when the nation's women were sacrificing their stylish bustles to make bandages, Mary greeted guests wearing wide-hoop dresses with impressive damask trains.

Absent in the press were stories of her daily visits to Union hospitals, where she composed letters for soldiers and comforted the suffering. Concerned about the incidence of scurvy among the patients, she donated $300 of her personal funds to purchase them fruit.

At the behest of her African-American dressmaker and confidant, Lizzie Keckley, Mary generously provided cash for bedding and other supplies needed by the Contraband Relief Society, which was formed to assist freed slaves who had migrated to Washington. Mary Todd Lincoln, the daughter of a slave owner, transcended the ugly institution of slavery and served the needs of people well before her husband, President Lincoln, earned the title of Great Emancipator.

Those curious to see Mary's decorator masterpiece were satisfied in February 1862, when the Lincolns hosted a sumptuous soiree to show off the refurbished White House. Mary was unable to fully enjoy compliments that night, however, as little Willie reclined upstairs on his sickbed. She repeatedly left the party to visit him, but a recovery would not come.

Willie's death sent Mary into a depression so deep that President Lincoln guided her to a window and pointed to the lunatic asylum in the distance, saying, "Try to control your grief, or it will drive you mad, and we may have to send you there."

In 1863, Mary's carriage overturned, tossing her so violently that she suffered a dangerous concussion from which some feel she never fully recovered. Erratic mood swings and debilitating headaches made her unpredictable. Once, in a rare public display of anger, she openly accused a general's wife of flirting with the president. Her loud accusations reached fever pitch until onlookers turned away, red faced. Lincoln was visibly pained by her words. The war had taken a toll on the country and on their marriage.

After Lincoln's reelection and the capture of Richmond in 1865, the pair felt some relief and levity, although Mary fretted over a terrifying dream that interrupted her husband's sleep; the image ended with his death.

On Good Friday, the Lincolns attended a play at Ford's Theater. Arriving late, they sat side by side in the Presidential Box. Mary affectionately sidled up to her sweetheart, clutching his hand like a new bride would her groom. Engrossed in the amusing dialogue, neither noticed the presence of John Wilkes Booth's gun until the president slumped away from his beloved seconds after a barely audible gunshot. It was Mary's screams that alerted the stunned audience that Lincoln's nightmare had come true. The patrons watched in horror as Mary desperately braced her wounded husband until help arrived. The critically injured president was quickly removed to a house across from the theater. Mary followed frantically. Her cries so bothered those attending Lincoln that she was unfairly banned from her dying husband's bedside.

Overwrought with grief at the death of her husband, Mary refused to leave her bed, sobbing so deeply that she suffered seizures. Again, friend Lizzie Keckley comforted her. Together, Mary and Lizzie sorted the president's artifacts and finalized the disposition to individuals Mary considered worthy of such memorabilia. Finally, after five weeks, Mary dressed in her finest black mourning clothes and left the national mansion without much notice. As she and youngest son Tad boarded a private rail car to Chicago, souvenir hunters entered the White House and irreverently pilfered swatches from the fine draperies, took the furniture, and confiscated the china that Mary had so carefully selected.

Almost immediately the widow Mary fixated on the fear that she would live a life of destitution. She penned urgent letters to senators begging for her widow's premium and pestered political friends and sponsors for donations. A secret plan to raise money by selling her clothes through New York brokers opened her up to cruel criticism about her taste in décolleté. Before she could settle her husband's estate, Mary found herself assailed by her enemies, and the "tell-all" accounts, whether true or fiction, made great reading.

Lincoln's former law partner, William Herndon, attempted to humiliate Mary by conducting a multi-city lecture series in 1866 where he sullied Lincoln's character with sensational claims. The alcoholic orator captivated audiences with purely invented, gossipy tales of Lincoln's purported love affair with a girl from his youth who had died before they could wed. Herndon slandered Mary, calling her a spendthrift, a madwoman, and a shrew. When Mary confronted him, he twisted her words and branded her a liar. To some, just raising the possibility made it seem true.

The betrayal continued with Lizzie Keckley's 1868 autobiography, which divulged private conversations between the Lincolns, disclosed intimate details of Willie's death, and discussed Mary's behind-closed-doors tirades. The revelations devastated Mary such that she denied ever knowing her former, trusted friend.

To avoid further humiliation, Mary and Tad traveled to Europe. While taking in the sights, Mary corresponded with friends and family. Through more than 600 letters still in existence, readers discover her generous, yet difficult personality. Nearly every week, Mary mailed her son Robert and his wife Mary Harlan scores of extravagant gifts, from gold pocket watches to diamond clusters; invariably, the packages were followed by letters in which she chastised them for not writing to her.

After a couple of years abroad, Mary and Tad returned to Chicago in 1871, and almost without warning, Tad contracted pleurisy and died. Anguished, Mary wrote, "Without Taddie I pray to die."

Mary took refuge in soothsayers and séances. During a stay in Florida, she experienced a series of disorienting episodes culminating in several incoherent telegraph messages to her only remaining son, Robert, whom she feared was ill. Mary rushed back to Chicago to monitor Robert's health, but shortly after her arrival, it became evident that it was *her* health that needed to be addressed.

Hotel staff told Robert of Mary's penchant for wandering the hallways half dressed and her routine requests to have a maid keep her company as she slept. As Mary teetered between rational and irrational thoughts, Robert made the painful decision to have her committed to an asylum.

Mother and son sat on opposite sides of a Cook County courtroom during the one-day trial that culminated in Mary's confinement to Bellevue Place in Batavia, Illinois. The apparent betrayal of her only son and the verdict of her peers pushed her over the edge. Court papers reveal that Mary was not considered dangerous, yet during her last night of freedom, she twice attempted suicide by drinking what she thought was laudanum, a substance she often mixed with camphor as part of her bath water. Her only saving grace came from an alert druggist who recognized her frail mental state and foiled her plan that very night by substituting sugar water in place of the dangerous drugs she requested. Robert learned of the incident and kept vigil by her bedside until morning, when the two took the train to Batavia.

Reluctant but composed, Mary rested in her first-floor hospital room and occasionally accepted short carriage rides into the countryside. Upon hearing of Mary's dilemma, longtime friends launched a vigorous campaign to free her. Robert, who was her court-appointed guardian, bowed under the pressure and agreed to permit his mother to leave the facility. On September 11, 1875, Mary was released to the care of her sister Elizabeth.

Back in Springfield, Mary stewed about Robert's court-sanctioned control of her money. The schism escalated as Mary wrote Robert threatening letters demanding the return of all gifts she had sent him, lest she pursue legal action that would notify the world of their break. The very private Robert was terrified of just such an indiscretion.

Eventually, the court cleared Mary of her insanity judgment, and Robert arranged to restore her wealth. Finally free, Mary sailed to Europe where she remained in personal exile until failing health forced her return to Illinois.

Mary reflected on the insanity episode, confiding to her sister that she realized her behavior was abnormal, but she felt that it stemmed from an accidental misuse of prescribed medications. Robert visited his mother at his aunt's home and delighted Mary by bringing her young granddaughter along. The gesture brought Mary and Robert a sense of reconciliation before her continued mental decline.

In the privacy of her upstairs chambers, an emotionally fragile Mary conducted a seemingly endless inventory of her collections, spending hours sorting expensive silks, admiring brand new gloves, and folding and refolding unworn shawls. She claimed to hear the president's voice and slept on one side of the bed so that he might join her.

When sixty-three-year-old Mary Lincoln crossed the veil of death on July 16, 1882, the *Chicago Tribune* casually placed the obituary in the middle column of page five. Elizabeth scoured the contents of Mary's sixty-four steamer trunks, but none held a suitable burial dress. The day before her funeral, America's misunderstood first lady lay in silent repose in the very room where she had married Abraham Lincoln forty years before, wearing the ring that he had given her and a plain white satin dress ordered from a catalog. After her death, her lifetime obsession with money proved ridiculous, as her estate held a value of over $90,000, including $72,000 in bonds.

At her funeral, the reverend described Mary and Abraham Lincoln as "two tall and stately pines standing on a rocky ledge where they had grown so closely together as to be virtually united at the base." One of the pines died from a lightning strike, while the other survived alone. He concluded, "When Abraham Lincoln died, she died. . . . So it seems to me today, that we are only looking at death placing its seal upon the lingering victim of a past calamity."

MYRA BRADWELL

1831–1894

Entrepreneurial Lawyer

SEATED BESIDE HER HUSBAND in the beautifully appointed parlor of their Michigan Avenue home, Myra Colby Bradwell entertained the *Chicago Daily Tribune* reporter with her usual panache. Later, the writer commented about Myra's bright brown eyes and dark brown hair, saying her "58 years rest upon her so lightly that she seems scarcely 40." Perhaps through work Myra had found Ponce de Leon's Fountain of Youth: She had challenged the United States Supreme Court, chaired a publishing dynasty, earned a fortune, and served as an ambassador for the city of Chicago, all while fulfilling the role of wife and mother. To Myra, activism was just part of her nature.

The Colbys were Yankees from Manchester, Vermont. They relocated to the Schaumburg, Illinois, area in 1843 when Myra was twelve years old. She was well liked and cited in the local paper for her popularity. Myra completed studies at the Elgin Female Seminary and settled into the profession of teaching, one of the few careers considered acceptable for women of the era. There were times, though, when her lively demeanor turned into a headstrong personality.

Myra's fierce independence culminated in her eloping with Englishman James Bradwell, whom she had known for mere months. Myra's family disapproved of the union and it is rumored that, in an attempt to dissuade the couple, one of her brothers chased them out of town with a shotgun.

As a wife, Myra fulfilled the womanly Victorian role dictated by the tenets of True Womanhood. She created a warm and inviting home, practiced her religion, selflessly supported her husband in his work, and wrapped her arms around numerous charitable causes. During this time she also became the mother of four children, of which only two survived.

During the Civil War, Myra chaired a committee for Chicago's Sanitary Commission Fair. Working side by side with nursing experts Mary A. Livermore and Jane C. Hoge, Myra helped raise more than $70,000 for the war effort and gained local celebrity. At war's end, she settled back into domesticity and reading law alongside her husband.

After several years it became obvious that she was qualified to sit for the law exam. In August 1869 she passed the Illinois Bar with highest honors. However, the exam results did not guarantee her the license to practice. That decision would be forthcoming after she petitioned the Illinois Supreme Court.

Myra anticipated that the governing body would scrutinize her request based on her gender. Hence, she bolstered her application with a quote from the Illinois Revised Statutes, clarifying that any individual described in "the masculine gender, females as well as males, shall be deemed to be included . . . showing no distinction between the sexes."

Much to her surprise, though, the court ignored her gender and instead rejected her based on her marital status. At the time, state law refused a married woman the right to enter into a legal contract without her husband's consent and signature. With such a restriction in place, a woman was essentially unable to conduct business. If Myra ignored this tenet, she might be arrested and charged with disobedience against the state.

Without hesitation, Myra appealed and this time received the result she had originally expected: She was denied admission by virtue of her gender. To circumvent her frustration, the justices of the Illinois Supreme Court included a four-point explanation.

First, as no woman in the state held the position of licensed attorney, the court stated there was a precedent prohibiting any and all women from practicing law. Second, true to the era, the court felt that because of "the delicacy" of a woman's emotional and physical constitution she would be unable to withstand the horror of certain types of cases. Third, they concluded that a female would have unfair advantage over a male because a jury would not be able to withstand the "mysterious wiles and charms of a woman lawyer."

As insulting as those excuses were, the fourth point probably covered the real reason for the ruling: There was concern that Myra's admission to the bar would spur an unbridled tidal wave of women into public service during an era when they were forbidden to vote. In other words, the topic at hand was one of suffrage.

Furious and more determined than ever, Myra turned to one of the nation's brightest legal minds. Senator Matthew H. Carpenter defended her position in front of the United States Supreme Court. In the case *Bradwell v. Illinois,* Carpenter attempted to steer the discussion away from women's suffrage and argued that women had the right to practice law without benefit of the right to vote. The Supreme Court was unimpressed, and in 1873 Myra was again denied admission to practice law in Illinois.

Associate Justice Joseph P. Bradley's words clearly echoed the views of the Victorian age: "The natural and proper timidity and delicacy which belongs to the female sex evidently unfits it for many occupations of civil life. . . . The paramount destiny and mission of

MYRA BRADWELL

women are to fulfill the noble and benign office of wife and mother. This is the law of the Creator."

Ironically, while Myra fought her case in the courts, the Illinois legislature passed a law giving all individuals the right to pursue any "occupation, profession, or employment (except military service) regardless of sex." It was a victory that opened the door to other women seeking admission to the Illinois Bar, but Myra, embroiled in her Supreme Court case, stubbornly refused to reapply for admission.

Instead, Myra concentrated on a new venture that allowed her to exercise her First Amendment rights. In 1868, the Illinois State Legislature passed a special proclamation authorizing her to start a newspaper that would publish recent court decisions, proposed laws, and new laws pending in the legislature. As publisher, editor, and business manager of the *Chicago Legal News,* Myra discovered her voice within its pages. In every issue she also included her own agenda on topics near to her heart, writing voluminous columns that addressed legal inequalities between the sexes.

Myra chastised universities for "favoring breeches over petticoats," saying, "Brains and mentality are measured by the formation of the wearing apparel. This will not do!" Called to task, schools began accepting women into their law programs, but there was a catch—and Myra didn't shy away from writing about the ostracizing methods implemented by unhappy faculty toward women students.

Women were often banned from daily classroom recitations and from using the law library with male students. At graduation, some women suffered the indignity of being relegated to the audience while their male counterparts sat smugly on stage. Men received their diplomas that day, while women were given theirs at a later date and only after they submitted a letter requesting the parchment.

Myra especially focused on licensing rules, since all lawyers needed one to practice in front of the courts. The inability to secure a license was the reason many remarkable female law graduates abandoned their dreams. Years later a Chicago newspaper commended Myra for her perseverance, saying, "She was content and pleased that other women reaped the fruits of her struggle to establish the equality of the sexes in the legal profession."

When she lobbied state officials to pass equality laws in Springfield, Myra was subtle in manner, sensing that flaming rhetoric might alienate lawmakers. The Illinois Press Association reported later that she combated objections "in a manner demonstrating both wisdom and discretion. Intuitively she seemed to read men's minds and conducted her warfare accordingly."

In 1869, Myra warned the female population against the use of radicalism to gain suffrage:

> You ask us, how shall this great privilege be obtained for women? We will tell you. Not by the class who term man "a tyrant"—but by the sensible and devoted mothers, wives, and daughters of the state unifying together, we mean those who have the respect and love of their fathers, husbands, and brothers, and asking them that they give to women the right to vote.

On the other hand, when Myra disagreed with judges, lawyers, and even the widely read *Chicago Tribune,* her dissenting opinion could be found in the *Legal News.* Sometimes her ladylike charms turned into justifiable rage. There was no pity for a judge or lawyer who particularly irritated her. Once she called an offending judge a "fossilized Bourbon Judge," and when another jurist callously embarrassed a woman lawyer in his courtroom, Myra not only printed his name but also his distasteful actions during the case. It was a form of censorship that worked on occasion. Judges, lawyers, and legislators roiled at the sight of their name printed in the *Legal News.*

As a respected businesswoman and mentor, Myra encouraged the dreams of others. Emma Frances Miller was one who benefited from Myra's direction. Emma described her first meeting with Myra in the "flickering light of a gas chandelier" within the offices of the *Chicago Legal News,* where she nervously shared her hope of becoming a reporter and asked Myra for a job. Not only did Myra give her an apprenticeship, which trained her in every task from gopher to proofreader, she also generously taught Emma every aspect of the business. Eventually, Emma was working in the composing room, where loud chugging machines transformed typeset copy into columns of inked characters and then onto giant rolls of newsprint. Myra also rewarded Emma's hard work with steady raises.

Myra believed that a dedicated worker deserved an excellent income, and those who did not meet her standards felt her wrath. Although she rewarded good work liberally, she was not immune to the popular protest tactics used by unions. Without much warning the Printer's Union declared a strike against the *Legal News.* However, union leaders misjudged the woman sitting behind the desk.

Perhaps her appearance lulled them into thinking they would have an easy victory. Myra dressed in lovely but formal black suits with ruffled lace scarves and accessorized with jet ear bobs and long, delicately beaded necklaces. However, the feminine attire belied her toughness. She confronted the union without sympathy. Rather than risk the reputation and deadline of her publication, Myra ceased talks and boldly hired "scabs" to complete the press run. At the conclusion of the strike, there was no doubt who was in charge.

There was one threat to Myra's enterprise that no one could have predicted. On October 8, 1871, the Bradwell family was awakened by a clamoring in the streets. Through the bedroom window, Myra saw the eerie glow of fire dancing in the distance. Grabbing some clothing and her pet bird, Myra guided the family into the street, where they joined neighbors and strangers alike in a human wave surging toward the safety of the lakefront.

Husband James and thirteen-year-old daughter Bessie paused at the offices of the *Legal News,* and Bessie collected her mother's address books of subscribers. Back in the street, father and daughter became separated. In the pandemonium Bessie ended up stranded on the other side of town. James was heartsick, but Myra, with her usual optimism, comforted her husband and son by saying, "I trust that girl to go to the ends of the earth. She'll come out all right, don't you worry." Myra's motherly instinct proved right, and Bessie was found the next day, toting her mother's heavy customer books with her. That gesture saved Myra's empire.

The Great Chicago Fire claimed an estimated 18,000 buildings. The Bradwells' home, James's law office, and Myra's *Chicago Legal News* building and printing facility sustained a total loss. Seemingly undaunted, Myra got right back to work. She arranged to have the *Legal News* published in Milwaukee, Wisconsin, and, amazingly, maintained her production schedule as though no calamity had occurred.

As the consummate businesswoman, she ran advertisements in the *Legal News* reminding lawyers and legislators that she had the ability to reprint documents destroyed in the fire. She knew firsthand that there would be a strong market for this service as the fire had claimed her own trove of over 2,000 volumes of what was thought to be the nation's largest private collection of law books.

Thanks to Myra's business, the Bradwells recovered from the disaster in good stead. They built a new three-story home with separate apartments on each floor so that their two adult children and families could reside with them. The publishing business was rebuilt, expanded, and upgraded with state-of-the-art printing technology. And Myra took on a new employee.

In his retirement, James took a secondary role in his wife's business. Again, as they had in younger years, they worked together: She had helped him by reading law, and now he assisted her with technical questions regarding the reproduction of photographs. The arrangement pleased Myra, as she believed "that married people should share the same . . . interests and be separated in no way." She once joked, "If [married couples] worked side by side and thought side by side we would need no divorce courts."

Myra constantly juggled business and personal demands. In 1875 Mary Todd Lincoln sent the Bradwells an urgent letter. The Bradwells and the Lincolns had been dear friends for many years, and after Lincoln's assassination the Bradwells helped the widow Lincoln to purchase a residence in their own neighborhood. When Mary's son, Robert Lincoln, placed her in a sanitarium, she turned to her friends for help. Myra immediately boarded a train to Batavia, Illinois, and demanded the hospital staff permit her to visit Mary. As one who understood how to manipulate the press, Myra then contacted newspaper editors, who were quite anxious for the juicy details surrounding the former first lady's situation. Within a few months, public pressure and the glare of embarrassment changed the minds of Robert Lincoln and the hospital's chief doctor. A suddenly sane and very grateful Mary Lincoln left the institution.

The city of Chicago also called on Myra. Chicago leaders were fixated on the heated national competition to snare the honor of host city for the world's fair. The event was timed to celebrate the 400th anniversary of Columbus' voyage to America, and city fathers felt Chicago, having risen from the ashes of the Great Fire of 1871 like the mythical Phoenix, could use the event to showcase to the world its miraculous transformation. As part of the legal committee to bring the Columbian Exposition World's Fair to the city, Myra lobbied fiercely, traveling to Washington to personally meet with legislators. Many in the United States government knew Myra since she had expanded the *Legal News* to include nationwide coverage of lawsuits and legislation, and her battles for equal rights were well publicized across the country. Her renown helped secure the bid for Chicago.

The city rejoiced when it was announced that it would host the Columbian Exposition World's Fair, but the Bradwells' joy was short-lived: Doctors informed Myra that she had cancer. Somehow the shocking diagnosis failed to unmoor her. She sailed to Europe and traversed the United States searching out the best treatments available. Whether it was the medications or sheer doggedness, Myra managed to survive, although in pain, for three years beyond the diagnosis. When the fair opened, she was able to tour the grounds for an entire week, riding in a wheelchair. Undoubtedly she was most satisfied by the wall of display cases containing early volumes of the *Chicago Legal News*.

As Myra faced death, there was one piece of unfinished business that James was bent on resolving. Unbeknownst to Myra, James had secretly requested that the state court admit Myra to the Illinois Bar without a formal application. The Illinois Supreme Court issued her license in 1890, and the United States Supreme Court followed two years later. Both recognized her status as retroactive to the date of her original application in 1869, giving her the honor of becoming the first woman lawyer in Illinois. Finally, she would have the privilege of signing the word "attorney" after her name.

When Myra received word of the decisions, she was deeply pleased, and, as would be expected, she printed the contents of both letters in the *Legal News* for all to read. Her greatest satisfaction, though, came from the knowledge that her life's work had removed barriers for the betterment of others. One of those who benefited from Myra's campaign was her own daughter Bessie, who became a licensed practicing attorney alongside her brother.

In her last months, Myra lay bedridden and weak in the sleeping chamber of the Bradwells' lavish Chicago home at 1428 Michigan

Avenue. Hoping to conserve her mother's strength, Myra's daughter Bessie did all to discourage visitors, but Myra overcame her protestations, saying, "Let me do all the good I can while I stay."

Days before her death, Myra relinquished her position at the helm of the *Legal News* to Bessie. The press lionized Myra in death, saying, "She didn't speak of sisterhood, she acted sisterhood."

During that rare 1889 interview with the *Chicago Daily Tribune* reporter, Myra reflected on the state of women. She said, "The world . . . has begun to learn the lesson that it is not necessary for a woman to break up all family ties and sacrifice womanly attributes and graces in order to succeed in other trades than the honored one of housewife."

Myra was a woman who truly had it all—a wildly successful career, wealth, good friends, and civic support. She was recognized throughout the nation for her tireless efforts to change the American legal system. But rather than those accomplishments, at the end of her life she spoke of the pride she felt for her family:

> I often wish all these excellent folk who used to picture me as a fanatic destroyer of domesticity and the sweetness of true womanhood could see . . . our home life. . . . All the wiseacres of the land made doleful prophecies concerning the end of my career when I signified my desire to become a lawyer by my application. They predicted that I'd wreck my family and break my hearthstone to smithereens. That was twenty years ago and I do not know of any other family whose integral character is so unbroken as mine.

DR. ELLA FLAGG YOUNG

1845-1918

Educational Stateswoman

Two hundred freshly scrubbed schoolchildren eagerly lined the aisles of Chicago's Auditorium Theater, anxiously raising their American Beauty roses to form a crimson floral arch. To the roar of applause, Dr. Ella Flagg Young entered the large room, passed beneath the flowers, and stepped onto the stage. The children followed her to the dais and laid their long-stemmed tributes at her feet, surrounding her with a fragrant carpet. The overflowing audience waited patiently as Ella returned her affection to each boy and girl by warmly shaking their hand.

As the community celebrated the completion of Ella's first year as superintendent of the Chicago schools, the nation still struggled with the idea that a woman served at the helm of the nation's second-largest school district. Indeed, at the time of her nomination on July 29, 1909, one school board member unabashedly expressed concern, saying, "I only wish Mrs. Young were a man."

That sentiment resonated throughout the United States. One magazine published a curt announcement of the sixty-four-year-old widow's appointment, saying, "Chicago has turned over the management of her $50,000,000 school system to a woman. She is, of course, an unusual woman, but all the same she is a woman and she has displaced a man." Fueled by early twentieth-century mores, the writer continued: "She is vigorous and alert, but it is quite certain that no man at that age would have been elected."

No matter age or gender, Ella was more than qualified for the position. During her acceptance speech before the Chicago Board of Education, she confidently voiced her stance:

> Women are destined to rule the schools of every city . . . In the near future we will have more women than men in the executive charge of the vast educational system. It is a woman's natural field, and she is no longer to do the greatest part of the work and yet be denied leadership. It will be my aim to prove that no mistake has been made and to show critics and friends alike that a woman is better qualified for this work than a man.

Ella prepared for leadership from her youngest days growing up in Buffalo, New York. Born on January 15, 1845, Ella thrived in her loving, middle-class family of five. Throughout her life, she possessed a unique ability to build on past knowledge and experiences.

Ironically, this woman, who ascended to head the Chicago schools, nearly missed out on a classroom education herself. Due to delicate health, Ella remained at home under the protection of her doting mother. Mrs. Flagg insisted that sun and fresh air suited her daughter better than the rigors of schoolwork. Ella typically spent her days obediently tending a garden parcel. Other times, she trailed along with her father to watch him work in the forge. By studying the laws of nature through the life cycle of plants and the step-by-step progression of manufacturing procedures, Ella developed critical thinking skills about the processes by which events occur. These lessons would serve her throughout her life.

DR. ELLA FLAGG YOUNG

The Flaggs' favorite pastime was reading, and books were abundant in the household. Surprisingly, no one urged Ella to read, and she showed no particular interest until one day when Mrs. Flagg shared a newspaper account of a schoolhouse fire in which several children had jumped from windows to escape the flames. The story traumatized nine-year-old Ella. She requested her mother reread the first few sentences, and, remarkably, with that knowledge she retreated to her room to decipher the words by applying sounds to the letters. It was as though the floodgates had opened.

Ella read voraciously, conquering titles tough for adults. Her new skill remained undetected until she shared the complex theories of Baxter's *Call to the Unconverted* with her mother's quilting group; the women sat flabbergasted. At age ten she taught herself to write. She also nagged her parents to allow her to attend school. The Flaggs relented and Ella shined as an exemplary student.

Within months of her thirteenth birthday, the Flagg family relocated to Chicago. Ella relished the opportunity to study there until the faculty informed her that she must complete one year in a Chicago grammar school before she would qualify for the high school examination. Trying to be a good sport, she dutifully accepted the rule and attempted to repeat the curriculum until boredom forced her to reconsider. She quit school, concentrating instead on home study.

Two years later, former classmates convinced Ella to take the teacher's examination. She passed the test, but was refused her teaching certificate on the grounds that she was too young. Superintendent Wells interceded for his stellar student, inviting Ella to pursue further studies at the Normal School. Here prospective teachers learned the standardized curriculums popular in pre–Civil War classrooms. Textbooks promoted rigid protocols, and there was little or no room for creativity. The level of mental stimulation appealed to Ella. However, after completing her first year at Normal, Mrs. Flagg intervened.

Ella tended toward perfectionism, and Mrs. Flagg felt this trait might color Ella's view of students. To ensure Ella realized that the needs of children superseded stuffy methods and formulas, Mrs. Flagg convinced her daughter to investigate the profession. It was from this frank discussion that the idea of student teaching emerged. Ella knocked on schoolroom doors in the quest to observe working classrooms.

One kind teacher encouraged Ella, permitting her to teach weekly lessons. The budding educator found herself reciprocating with fondness for the young students. Impressed by Ella's transformation, Mrs. Flagg became her biggest supporter.

After graduation in 1862, seventeen-year-old Ella accepted employment as a primary teacher at Chicago's Foster School. The thrill she felt, as she stepped onto the wide-planked flooring of her own classroom for the first time, was subdued by the sudden death of her very proud mother just two weeks later.

School administrators took early note of their new teacher. Ella's first assignment was short-lived, as within the month she was tapped to corral a group of rowdy characters nicknamed the "cowboy class." These farm kids didn't faze Miss Flagg.

Many of Ella's seventy-seven students towered over her petite 5-foot frame. She refused to be intimidated by the heavier and oft-times older pupils. Ella's lack of an early classroom education proved an asset. She approached pupils with directness, and this personable interaction fired her students into model performers. One student described Miss Flagg as "all vim, push, and go-ahead." She added, "My, how she would make those boys fly." Another former pupil wrote, "I always call her our principal in speaking of my school days for I loved her dearly then and still love her."

In just one year, Ella was promoted to head assistant of the Brown School. Her salary doubled to $500 monthly, and her classroom was downsized to fifty-six students to allow her time to complete administrative tasks. Next she served as the principal of the Practice School. Her dedication to the school was undeniable, but Ella understood the need to balance one's life.

Privately, in her hotel home, Ella devised a tool of personal discipline that she called "systematic work." Within this process she devoted three evenings to study and three evenings to visiting friends and performing community service. Sunday remained for religious expression. This foundation taught her efficiency.

Ella became a bride in December 1868, marrying Chicago merchant William Young. Sadness had haunted her earlier that year when her only brother was killed in a freak train accident. Sorrow struck again in 1873 when her ailing husband died and her beloved father and older sister succumbed to the influenza epidemic. She countered her loneliness by diving into her work, surrounding herself with her students.

Within three years, Ella contemplated the decision to become principal of the struggling Skinner School. Again, she didn't jump at the promotion but analyzed the challenges first. She realized that at this level she would be scrutinized by everyone from the mayor to the general public. She felt she was up to the task.

Ignoring the pressures, Principal Ella Young boldly eliminated corporal punishment and permitted teachers leeway within the classroom, saying, "No one can work in another's harness." Teachers appreciated the freedom. Parents were pleased by the regular contact she and her staff maintained with them, and the administration supported her concepts. Ella eliminated homework, maintaining that learning should be conducted under a teacher's guidance. The students were delighted.

She donated her own books to create one of the first public school libraries in the city and invited teachers to meet in her home to discuss popular educational topics. The results of her leadership were spectacular. Mayor Harrison called Ella's Skinner School, "the most effective social institution in the city." Some board members determined that Ella was "too big a woman for her present place" and suggested that she "was wanted for a bigger job."

Her role expanded to the assistant superintendent. She relished the opportunity and commenced to create an atmosphere of optimal learning. She also adeptly monitored the politics within the school system, a lesson that would serve her later.

Social movements in labor and suffrage spilled into the streets, influencing decisions that impacted education. Practical classes to train children in life skills were considered by some to be fads. Teachers felt pressure in crowded classrooms. Ella rode the wave of controversy with tenacity. Those who performed to her standards were applauded, and those who lacked focus received no mercy. Physically the job was immense, but her role was about to expand yet again. The governor appointed her to the Illinois Board of Education in 1889, giving her wider recognition among educators, who teased her as the "best man on the board." She craved the next step.

Realizing that superintendents held doctorates, she toyed with the possibility of attending the University of Chicago. Bickering among the board of education, teacher's organizations, city politicians, and Superintendent Andrews gave her the perfect window of opportunity to resign from her twelve-year assignment as assistant superintendent.

In 1889, she joined the university staff as an associate professor of pedagogy under the tutelage of John Dewey. Educational theories such as Dewey's "Pragmatism," which analyzed the best way to teach students based on human behaviors and an individual's ability to solve problems, spawned a renaissance of social activism in the classroom. Ella already incorporated pieces of this precept into her teaching. She vigorously challenged Dewey's ideas, causing him to later acknowledge that Ella's incessant questions had driven him to refine his applications. It was with this same ardor that Ella designed her own theories of education.

Her dissertation, titled *Scientific Method in Education,* discussed how to translate scientific methods into classroom experiences. She explained that students are individuals, each with their own ways of learning, understanding, and performing a task. Ella also stressed that all schools should be run in a democratic way with inclusion of all students desiring an education.

She was awarded her degree in 1900 and settled into the position of Professor of Education at the University of Chicago. It's possible that she would have finished her career teaching the finer details of the English language if it weren't for the political landscape at the university.

Tensions mounted between Ella and her department chairman and mentor John Dewey when students ranked her classes superior to his. Next, professors, who contributed research for Dewey's books on educational theory, became incensed when he failed to give them proper recognition, and by virtue of her close camaraderie with Dewey, Ella found herself in the middle of a battle of egos. When Dewey became mired in intrigue over a university-sponsored experimental elementary school, Ella was selected to be the spokesperson for the project, causing some to call her Dewey's shill. Ella felt pressure to protect her reputation and did so by resigning from the university. She sailed for Europe, leaving Dewey to deal with the problems that he'd created.

During her year's hiatus, she monitored Chicago's education drama from afar and waited for the best time and opportunity to present itself before retuning to the states. Within a short time of her arrival home, Ella found herself being wooed to assume the principal's job at the Chicago Normal School. The offer was perfect and would allow Ella to test her dissertation theories as she wished.

Once installed as principal, she set about to roll back twenty-five years of dogma. This dismantling and reconstruction of the Normal School's educational system became a template for what could be done on a larger scale within the Chicago schools. Any doubts of her abilities were quickly swept away. Her masterful repair of the broken system positioned her as a candidate for the top job when the superintendent of Chicago schools retired in 1909.

Although her record proved her capable, the school board dragged its feet for the next five months. They would not consider her their only candidate, and to Ella's credit, she told confidants that she would not accept the superintendent's position unless she was more than a figurehead: She expected to be given power to make decisions without being second-guessed.

Five candidates interviewed for the top job and Ella was the only woman in the group. When her appointment was announced, even the media showed a new respect for her by calling her Dr. Young. The $10,000 salary made her the highest-paid woman in the public service sector. As superintendent, she implemented many ground-breaking programs.

Drawing on her own childhood illness, she arranged for infirm students to enjoy open-air time and implemented special needs programs for handicapped pupils. Ella's commitment to physical health drew the ire of some when she created "personal purity" classes designed to teach sex education to boys and girls in segregated health classes.

She supported gardening in classrooms so that children could witness the growth process from seed to harvest. Believing that schools should serve all students under one roof, she incorporated vocational, manual arts, and technical training as companion courses to the standard curriculum.

During her administration, she formed teachers' councils to guarantee that educators had a voice at school board meetings and within the Chicago Teachers Federation. When budget shortfalls were announced, Ella bravely told teachers they would be expected to work for two weeks without pay, and she knocked heads with the likes of Jane Addams when the noted social activist interfered with teachers' negotiations for a raise. Even with long hours and high demands, Ella never lost the personal touch that she valued herself. It is said that she knew the names of each of the 6,000 teachers under her.

At the conclusion of her first year as superintendent, Ella was elected the president of the Illinois State Teacher Association, she was feted by the teachers in a grand celebration at the Auditorium Theater, and on June 15, 1910, the University of Illinois awarded her an honorary doctorate degree of law.

All of this notoriety drew the attention of the Chicago teacher organizations that saw her as the perfect candidate for the presidency of the National Educators Association (NEA). The leaders within the organization were running amok and feared the unionization of its members. Ella agreed to run.

Supporters rallied, sporting buttons that said "Young and Active." As part of her platform, she investigated the NEA's "permanent fund," which appeared mysteriously deficient in cash flow. Ella was elected the organization's first female president in 1910, but her campaign activities brought her anonymous death threats.

Meetings prior to the NEA national convention were heated and acrimonious. By the time Ella boarded the train to San Francisco, her emotions were out of check. The impending showdown over the old guard's handling of the treasury caused her to break out in shingles. The intolerable bouts of gnawing pain forced her to sleep suspended in a hammock fixed inside her berth.

Once in California, the NEA membership's rousing reception boosted her confidence. With teachers' support, she masterfully manipulated the voting bloc to force resignations from the unsympathetic long-time officers. The event was a complete success. She had demonstrated her diplomacy skills with her trademark sarcasm and humor. By the end of her year as NEA president, Ella finally confirmed her hunch about the misplaced funds. They had been squandered through bad investments. Her job was finished.

Back home in Chicago, there was more work to be done. Politics dominated negotiations surrounding pensions, causing a rift between Ella and the teachers. Arguments over textbooks, curriculum, and the balance of power continually strained all affected parties.

When the board balked at renewing Ella's contract, she resigned, forcing them to vote for her retention. A second confrontation regarding her contract took place in December 1913, but this time the board ousted Ella, triggering a media and public frenzy.

Stinging from the board's betrayal, she refused all calls, allowing only her closest friends to join her at home. One friend wrote of Ella's reaction, saying, "She cried enough tears to wash away all the sins of the world."

Public outcry brought about investigations, which uncovered an orchestrated conspiracy to remove Ella. Eventually, she was reinstated. However, the attempted ouster caused embarrassment and sore feelings on the part of the participants. Those board members who didn't agree with Ella's resuming her position continued to drag their feet and dog her agenda, grinding business to a virtual halt. Factions splintered and derailed her best efforts to heal the group into a smoothly working team. Wearied by the fighting, Ella knew that the time for retirement had come.

In December 1915, after six and a half years as the superintendent, Ella stepped down. Laurels poured in from all over the country. After the final banquet, Ella returned home quietly and closed her front door. For the first time in over a half century, she was a normal citizen, no longer employed as a servant of the people. She was now free to come and go as she pleased.

Ella briefly traveled to California, and with the advent of World War I, she campaigned tirelessly on behalf of the Liberty Loan Committee, selling bonds to support the war chest. It was this generous donation of time that probably cost her life.

While on the road, she was exposed to the Spanish flu. Seventy-three-year-old Ella died on October 26, 1918, while in Washington, D.C. Her body was returned to Chicago, where the city's flags flew at half-staff and black draperies covered the doorway at City Hall and the Board of Education. However, quarantine regulations dictated that burials be immediate, so citywide observances were cancelled. Instead, one hundred dearest friends and associates mourned her at Rosehill Cemetery. The Illinois Reserve Militia escorted her modest entourage, reflecting the words of the U.S. Secretary of the Treasury, who commended her for "working as a soldier."

Upon her death, one official shortsightedly wrote: "Had she been a man . . . [she] would have . . . commanded an army." In many ways she did command an army, but that contingent consisted of children who loved her, teachers who respected her, and a grateful public at large.

JANE ADDAMS

1860–1935

Social Pacifist

JANE SNUGGLED THE CHILDREN AROUND HER CHAIR and waited for their quiet attention before opening the book on her lap. She was never a teacher, but she was often seen instructing little ones. She was never a mother, but some called her the Mother of Peace. Over the course of forty-eight years, she used her own resources to improve the lot of thousands and became the first American woman to win the Nobel Peace Prize. To Jane Addams work was merely the manifestation of the Victorian principle of a "useful life."

She was born September 6, 1860, as Laura Jane Addams, a formal moniker that quickly gave way to the pet name Jennie. The family lived in the frontier Illinois town of Cedarville in Stephenson County, on a pleasant hillside along the trickling creek bed of the highly exaggerated Cedar River. Jane's parents settled there in 1844 and ran a mill that, combined with John Addams's speculator investments in the fledgling railroad, generated a handsome income.

Bright and precocious are two words commonly used by historians to describe the youngest daughter of Sarah and John Huy Addams. Her biographer and nephew, James Weber Linn, writes of his aunt's remarkable mind with which, as a youngster, she exercised her father's views on topics from theology to politics. She also appeared to have a gift for recollection, as she remembered standing beside her mother's deathbed at the age of two and a half.

It was natural that after the passing of her mother, Jane gravitated toward her remaining parent. All agree that she adored her father and relied on him as her beacon and guiding force. John fostered his daughter's intellectual hunger, although such deep thinking became a feature of her personality that caused her great consternation.

In her first autobiography, *Twenty Years at Hull-House,* Jane shared her ominous childhood sense of personal responsibility for the welfare of the world. As she explained, recurring dreams placed her as the only human who could save the world, if only she could successfully build a wagon wheel. The horror behind the nightmare stemmed from her realization that, as a six-year-old girl, she had not acquired such a skill, thus the world was doomed. The urgency of the task lingered over her daily thoughts at a time of life when a normal child would be focused on play.

Jane also fretted over the poverty of others. She noticed that, as the daughter of an Illinois state senator and prominent businessman, she wore a lovely coat to church while some children in church had no coat at all. On an errand with her father, she studied the tenements along the streets and alleys of Freeport and told her father that one day she would return to have "a big house built right in the middle of [the] horrid little houses" where the poor might have a sanctuary. At the tender age of eight, she had just effectively foreshadowed her future work.

According to biographer Linn, Jane's life lightened considerably at age eight, when her father married the widow Anna Haldeman. It wasn't the introduction of a new mother that eased her serious nature, but Anna's two boys—in particular George, who was

JANE ADDAMS

about the same age as Jane. The pair became ready playmates, running the acres of the Addams farm, creating dramas, killing snakes, and exploring caves. Jane and George shared a strong affection for each other, causing Anna to hope for a marriage. Although George considered such a proposal, Jane did not. She was content to read and think and concentrate on her education. Unlike most girls of the Victorian era, she had no fear of becoming a spinster.

Upon graduating from high school, Jane set her sights on a degree from Smith College in Northampton, Massachusetts. She passed the oral entrance exam, but her father interposed, informing her that instead she would attend nearby Rockford Female Seminary, where he was a member of the Board of Trustees. Disappointed, she quietly respected his wishes.

The atmosphere at the all-woman school tended to be more religious than scholarly. Jane served as class president and agitator in residence, testing the theology and the patience of the school's founder. Jane was particularly bent on having the institution change its name to Rockford College and confer academic degrees, as was provided for in the school's original charter. The administration was content to provide a certificate of graduation.

Her constant negotiations resulted in victory, and a year after her satisfactory matriculation, she was awarded the A.B. degree she had so coveted. At the time she described herself as "already beginning to emerge from that rose-colored mist with which the dream of youth so readily envelopes the future." But before she emerged from that rose-colored mist, she was to receive a devastating shock.

John Addams suddenly fell ill and died in August 1881 while on a family excursion. Jane, George, and Anna were all witnesses to the tragic event. He left an estate in excess of $350,000. Before his death, he had arranged for Jane to continue her education. Heartbroken as she was, she again followed his direction.

At age twenty-one, and just two months after her loss, Jane registered at the Woman's Medical College in Philadelphia, Pennsylvania. The class work busied her, but only deferred the grieving process. In the spring of 1882, the residue of unresolved emotional and physical pain caught up with her, and she suffered a nervous breakdown. After a hospitalization in Philadelphia, she returned to Illinois and then to Iowa, where her brother-in-law, a noted physician, performed a radical surgical procedure on her curved spine.

A year of recuperation followed, providing Jane the luxury of her favorite pastime: reading. At the end of the summer of 1883, she boarded a ship with her stepmother and sailed to Europe for a two-year respite. There she spent relaxed days admiring the art and architecture of France, England, Italy, and Germany.

During this first trip Jane witnessed the abject poverty of London's notorious East Side, where paupers bargained for rotting food lest they suffer the fate of starvation. The image haunted her. It was the turning point that set her thoughts percolating toward a solution. Jane later described these nomadic years with a quote by Tolstoy: She was in the midst of "the snare of preparation."

Upon her arrival in the United States, Jane entertained family and friends, but her heart was not in the socializing. It was time for her to escape from what she called the "dupe of deferred purpose." Certain of her path, she set out to change the world.

Returning to England with Rockford Seminary friend Ellen Gates Starr, Jane visited Toynbee Hall, a settlement established in London in 1844 by Arnold Toynbee. The arrangement of university-educated people sharing culture with the poor gave Jane a vision. As explained in her autobiography, she would involve college women "who had been smothered and sickened with advantages" and were seeking a way of meaningful service to others.

Back home her concept received little support from surprised family members. Undaunted, Jane plodded forward, adjusting her finances, taking lessons in bookkeeping, and searching out a Chicago neighborhood suitable for her venture.

The five-month project to find a building began in January 1889. A solid-looking, redbrick home built in 1856 by Charles J. Hull caught Jane's eye, but the meandering Chicago roads surrounding it confused her so that she was unable to find it again for several days. Finally, she stumbled upon the impressive structure with its wraparound wooden porch and striking presence on the street. The address then was 335 South Halsted and, although it needed some renovation, the location in Chicago's Nineteenth Ward was superior as it was surrounded by colonies of immigrant families from Russia, Italy, Greece, and Poland. The home looked much like the one she had pictured as a child: a stately old mansion among "horrid little houses."

Before her thirtieth birthday, Jane signed the lease with Helen Culver, the owner of the home. Rent was set at $60 per month. After cleaning and repairing the property, Jane and Ellen Gates Starr embarked on the great experiment, opening Hull House on September 18, 1889.

Hull House guests were warmly welcomed, and often it was Jane, wearing a finely tailored, long black dress, who greeted them. Sometimes she had a book in her hand or a baby on her hip. She treated all guests as equals. For years she resided in a modest but comfortable apartment in the second story of Hull House.

In its inaugural year, the settlement accommodated requests from over 9,000 people, but the initial plan of introducing culture to the immigrant population soon became secondary to the immediate needs of the people. There were urgent requests for a day nursery and a kindergarten that would encourage early education. Classes filled quickly, forcing many to sign up on a long waiting list.

The female residents and volunteers shared their knowledge freely. They provided lessons in music, art, cooking, and needlework.

Skills like bookbinding, typing, and dressmaking were taught, and literature discussions were popular. Speakers such as architect Frank Lloyd Wright and education innovator John Dewey lectured to eager audiences.

By 1907 the Hull House development consisted of thirteen buildings, including a gymnasium; theater; music school; coffee house; pool; clubhouses for men, women, boys, and girls; an art gallery; and studios. There was a post office, a large public kitchen with stoves and ample hot water, a spacious dining area, and even indoor bathtubs. Many of the immigrants lacked such luxuries in their own homes. Those things aside, one of the most important aspects of Hull House was Jane's insistence that it be a safe haven where guests could experience the freedom of being themselves and share their cultural pride without fear of ridicule or criticism. It was a kindness that they did not receive at their jobs or in the greater community.

Believing in the power of the pen, Jane wrote extensively on the problems of poverty. Throughout her autobiographies, she discusses the dangerous health threats faced daily by immigrants residing in filthy tenements. Debilitating and often fatal diseases, such as tuberculosis and typhoid fever, spread easily among the vulnerable population. Jane crusaded for better housing, contacting politicians and landlords to correct deficiencies in overcrowded buildings. In some cases she fought to have unsafe structures razed. Fighting city hall was never part of Jane's original vision for Hull House, but problems needed to be addressed, and she willingly took on the mantle of extremist in situations where she could exact results.

Jane's vigorous complaints about the miserable job done by trash collectors in her ward garnered her the appointment as Chicago's first female garbage inspector, a position that paid $1,000 a year and required her attention at 6:00 every morning. Once in a while she climbed from her "garbage phaeton" to do the dirty work herself. The neighbors appreciated her tenacious fight for change.

Just as Hull House attracted those in need, it also appealed to those who wanted to assist. Dedicated and determined women like Julia C. Lathrop (who became the United States Children's Bureau Director), labor leaders Florence Kelly, Alzina Parsons Stevens, and Mary Kenney, and medical researcher Dr. Alice Hamilton provided valuable resources for the settlement community.

Many of the seventy residents conducted studies to identify problems, then pushed for regulations to improve conditions and the quality of life for women and children. Their findings galvanized the judicial system to develop legal safeguards for children by creating the nation's first juvenile court and a support system for those youth accused of crimes though the Juvenile Psychopathic Clinic and the Juvenile Protective Association. The examination of abuses in the workplace led to the passage of Illinois laws that stipulated the hours, age limit, and types of work that women and children might do. These laws would become the model for future federal protection acts.

Word of the successes at Hull House spread throughout the country, and at the turn of the century, more than one hundred settlements served the nation. Chicago, much enthused by the good results, supported thirty-five enclaves sponsored by churches or private groups. Hull House served as America's premier example, and Jane found herself and her expertise in demand.

Whether or not it was Jane's intention, she found herself in the middle of the Progressive Era of social action. It was a time when people were organizing and demanding improved conditions. She was selected to negotiate during arbitrations between businesses, workers, the city, and the residents. Her participation was not always appreciated. For instance, the requirement of compulsory education for children and limitation of work hours for women often had the net effect of imposing a financial strain on families in desperate need of that income.

Her growing popularity and power threatened politicians and businessmen. She was mocked with the title "Saint of the Slums" and criticized as unpatriotic and a danger to the economy. Her radical opinions and staunch support of social welfare legislation prompted Delaware representative Thomas Bayard to take the floor of the United States Congress in 1926 and accuse her of having dangerous motives, saying that she "and Hull House can campaign for the most radical movements, with hardly a breath of public suspicion."

The words of others didn't appear to affect Jane. By 1915, with the expansion of America's role in World War I, Jane's speeches became more controversial. After a lecture in New York, angry letters flooded newspapers nationwide, calling her ignorant and uneducated. The bad press threatened the financial support of skittish Hull House backers. However, not everyone abandoned the cause. Others, like Chicago socialite Louise Bowen, applauded Jane's proactive views and generously donated more than $750,000 to Hull House during her lifetime.

At the conclusion of the war, Jane expanded her activism to international politics. Between 1922 and 1923, she commenced a world tour, addressing women's issues from podiums in South America, the Philippines, Germany, Russia, and Poland. Her fame was not lost on the people of Japan, where the press identified her as the "Mother of Peace."

She campaigned for women's suffrage and held office in numerous organizations. Groups like the National Association for the Advancement of Colored People and the American Civil Liberties Union benefited from her sway. It was, however, her foray into pacifism at the beginning of World War I that seemed to dominate her focus.

She founded the Women's Peace Party, renamed the Women's International League for Peace and Freedom in 1919, and served as their first president. Later in 1929, the members voted her Honorary President for Life.

By now she had outlived her friend Ellen Star Gates and close confidant Mary Rozet Smith. Jane herself suffered from heart disease and cancer, yet she stopped by Hull House with some regularity, having taken residence outside of Hull House some years before.

News of her election to receive the 1931 Nobel Peace Prize arrived shortly before her fifth surgery. The crusader of nearly fifty years was unable to attend the ceremony in Oslo, Norway, but it genuinely pleased her to be selected. There were other distinctions, too: She was conferred honorary doctorate degrees from fourteen universities and had been recognized with proclamations, cash awards, plaques, and statues. The scope of her influence spanned the globe, far from quaint Cedarville and the family farm where Jane had once played with her brother under the Norway spruces planted by her father.

Jane died of cancer at age seventy-five on May 21, 1935.

Up until her death, some still considered her the "most dangerous woman in the United States." The criticism did little to dissuade those who frequented Hull House. More than 2,000 thankful citizens attended her funeral, many sobbing uncontrollably.

Jane is buried in a modest grave in Cedarville, Illinois. One might expect an impressive stone monument. Instead, Jane rests in the family plot beneath an unpretentious marker with the following inscription:

JANE ADDAMS

OF

HULL HOUSE

AND THE

WOMEN'S INTERNATIONAL LEAGUE

FOR

PEACE AND FREEDOM

After her passing, Hull House forged on for more than twenty-eight years until 1963 when, after a protracted court battle, the Illinois Supreme Court upheld Chicago's right to condemn the hundred-acre site as a "slum clearance area." The ruling made way for the city to demolish the complex. The campus of the University of Illinois at Chicago now stands in its place.

Today, two of the original settlement buildings remain: the dining hall and the Charles J. Hull mansion. The latter has been restored to its earlier splendor and is protected as a National Historic Landmark and museum dedicated to the memory of Jane Addams.

ANNIE MINERVA TURNBO POPE MALONE

1869-1957

Rare Millionaire

ANNIE TUCKED A RING OF BRASS KEYS into the trembling hands of her secretary. The keys would open the door to a new home that Annie had purchased for her loyal employee. This wasn't the first time Annie heaped lavish gifts upon a worker. She felt it was the least she could do to reward her staff for their dedication. Annie generously shared her fortune with others, and she wouldn't have it any other way.

The mainspring of Annie Minerva Turnbo's philanthropy stemmed from her personal experience of growing up poor in post–Civil War black America. Both of her Kentucky-born parents had survived the bonds of slavery. Mother Isabella escaped to freedom while father Robert served as a Union soldier. After the war, the Turnbos settled in Illinois, where their small farm in the "Colored Town" section of the southern village of Metropolis overlooked the rushing Ohio River.

The Turnbos were hard-driven, churchgoing Republicans. Little Annie was months away from completing first grade at the Livingston Institute School when her parents died, leaving eleven orphaned

ANNIE MINERVA TURNBO POPE MALONE

children to scatter among relatives. During this time, Annie became fascinated by an elderly aunt who practiced herbal medicine. It was an interest that would serve Annie well in years to come.

At age fourteen, Annie moved to Peoria to live with a sister. There she enrolled in high school and discovered a passion for chemistry. Her studies were curtailed by an eye affliction that substantially dimmed her eyesight. She weathered the setback by borrowing science books from helpful teachers. When she wasn't engaged in reading, she immersed herself in her next favorite pastime: hairdressing.

The art of hair design suited Annie's quiet, patient, and serious personality. She impressed her sister's friends and neighbors with her knowledge and skill, but when she shared her hope of earning an income from the beauty trade, they argued the impracticality of her choice. Certainly, they spoke from experience.

In the 1880s, very few job options were available to women, and women of color were especially challenged to find work outside of a laundry, field, factory, or kitchen. Annie ignored the advice, concentrating instead on developing herbal and acorn balms.

Annie tested the effectiveness of her concoctions on a stray cat suffering from mange. Several mixtures improved the cat's raw skin. She analyzed the reaction of sunlight on germinating seeds and decided to test heat on the skin to see if it stimulated hair growth. Having witnessed the rejuvenating effects of Annie's methods, her sister became an enthusiastic supporter and even helped by monitoring Annie's simmering potions. Human experimentation yielded Annie's first payday when one satisfied woman voluntarily paid 25 cents for a treatment.

The evolution of Annie's *Wonderful Hair Grower* took more than a decade. Besides selling the product door to door, word of mouth brought a stream of regular customers to her sister's Peoria home. Annie realized that, although business was steady, it might be expanded if she relocated to a town with a larger black community. Annie had just such a place in mind.

The prominently African-American town of Lovejoy (Brooklyn), Illinois, was situated 6 miles from St. Louis, Missouri. After developing a budget, Annie rented the backroom of a modest wood-frame building for $5.00 a month. Then, with no formal training in sales techniques, she knocked on every door in town. If there was interest, she demonstrated the products on herself. She also discussed the importance of hygiene and cleanliness. Not everyone was convinced.

Initially, she encountered some skepticism. After all, many of her potential clients had suffered terrible outcomes with other products claiming similar results. They'd been burned before, literally, by harsh lye-based shampoos sold with the promise to straighten black hair. Why would this product be any different?

Annie overcame their objections with her calm, professional manner. She always dressed nicely in a proper walking suit, and her clean hair was neatly pinned in a sleek, neat style. As a black woman she understood their fears. She explained that she was selling her own proven formula rather than a brand made by a white manufacturer for the black marketplace. Her pitch and product boosted confidence. Within a year, at the dawn of the twentieth century, she realized her dream of full-time employment in the hair-care business.

In 1900, Annie patented a steel hot comb. The popular tool featured widely spaced teeth that allowed it to glide through hair to smooth its texture. With the introduction of the comb and a brisk demand for her goods, Annie became keenly aware that just months after her move, she was unable to manage all aspects of her business. It was time to take the next crucial step.

Before the end of her first year in Lovejoy, Annie hired three saleswomen, and following a business model similar to that used by the California Perfume Company (Avon), she formulated a sales program where each employee earned a commission on every item they sold. With staff in place, Annie again considered market expansion. Newspaper accounts about the upcoming Louisiana Purchase Exposition World's Fair in St. Louis, Missouri, intrigued her. The possibility of gaining national and worldwide contacts sealed the deal.

The fair was scheduled to open in 1903 but was delayed for a year. Annie, on the other hand, did not wait. She settled in a small apartment in the black neighborhood at Market Street and immediately entered St. Louis's teeming streets with her case containing hair treatments, non-toxic face powder, cleanser, tetter (skin-disease) relief, and moisturizer.

Perhaps her most important visits were to the construction sites surrounding the fairground complex. Here, thousands of laborers lived along the fringe of the grounds in a place called Forest Park. As the men toiled in hard labor, black women provided the basic needs of food and clean laundry. Annie saw this as an opportunity to recruit workers and expand into other states, as many of the camp women were southern transplants who had family back home. The plan worked.

With names and addresses in hand, Annie next boarded a train for a nine-month tour of the Deep South. It wasn't a journey for the faint of heart. African-Americans found 1905 Mississippi far from friendly. Lynching was a constant threat. Education was lax and illiteracy high. What Annie witnessed shocked her. As she once observed to an associate, "Slavery ended 40 years earlier, but black people still lived like slaves."

Knocking on the doors of shanties, Annie was an anomaly with her finely polished appearance. Typically, she found herself facing a woman wearing a faded cotton dress peeking from beneath a stained apron, looking burdened and older than her years. At every home Annie heard the same story repeated from their lips: Dawn found them already sweating in the field before going to a day job as a domestic, and then returning home to a family anxious for a morsel of food.

Annie must have seemed like an angel as she washed their hair and told them they could defeat poverty and become self-reliant. Her visits created a buzz in the community and several suggested that she show her products at a church meeting. Annie had always spoken with one woman at a time, but she agreed to meet with the women congregants. She was amazed when nearly two dozen women gathered to view the demonstration; eleven of them signed on as new representatives.

Poverty in the black community made Annie's proposition attractive. In 1900, the average salary in the United States was 22 cents an hour. In 1910, a domestic worker earned about $2.00 per week. With Annie's products the potential for income greatly exceeded those numbers. Back in Illinois and Missouri, her agents were banking between $3.00 and $5.00 a day, and several earned a staggering $100 a week. The math was advantageous to Annie as well. By 1911, a tin of preparation cost 2½ cents to manufacture, Annie sold it to her saleswomen for 25 cents, and they in turn sold it to consumers for 50 cents, making a nice profit for everyone.

During her Southern excursion Annie comprehended the power of group meetings. The concept of forming a school to simultaneously teach students began to percolate. Annie believed in education and saw financial independence as the key to solving problems. Annie felt good about the progress she'd made, but her success brought a challenge from an unexpected source.

One of her former saleswomen had resigned to market her own hair product, which she boldly named the same as Annie's *Wonderful Hair Grower*. Annie moved swiftly to trademark a company name and patent her products to avoid further infringement. She selected the African word PORO, which means "devotional society."

The mission of her company began to crystallize beyond expanding the business and making money. It became a form of religion, empowerment, personal responsibility, and politics.

Annie planned to aggressively introduce PORO to the public in 1904. No African-American woman had ever before called together the national black media for a news conference, so they were surprised when Annie took the podium. By the end of the meeting, the reporters understood that Annie expected PORO to change the potential of black women and the community at large. Next she tackled advertising.

As early as 1890, publications featured the wistful gaze of Charles Gibson's illustrations. The "Gibson Girl" image of the finely coiffured lady influenced women for a generation, including women of color who searched for the magic remedy to reproduce the look. At the suggestion of Chicago newspaper magnate Claude Barnett, Annie set out to alter the black ideal with the help of noted African-American artist Charles C. Dawson.

Readers of black-owned publications found themselves admiring Dawson's elegant portraits of familiar faces. The thin-lipped, European-looking girl was gone. So were the unflattering caricatures of African-American women, with exaggerated facial features and unkempt hair.

PORO advertisements featured beautifully dressed black women replete with dazzling jewelry and stylish hair. Men wore dapper suits and leaned against expensive cars. Another PORO rendering depicted a modern black woman encircled by a montage of lovely women from Africa wearing traditional ancestral headdresses and hairstyles. The drawings elicited a sense of heritage and pride previously neglected in black advertising. The response to PORO was tremendous. The public understood Annie's message. Women clamored to be sales agents, and the demand for Annie's products increased substantially.

As a black woman in segregated America, Annie's options for sales were limited. She was barred from conducting business with drugstores, and retailers refused to carry her line. PORO's success stemmed from the efforts of door-to-door saleswomen and PORO beauty salon owners who ran shops in their homes or neighborhoods. Some believe that Annie was the nation's first African-American woman to become a millionaire. By the mid-1920s, Annie claimed a worth of $14 million.

The ultimate dream of building a cosmetology school came true in 1918 when Annie opened PORO College. She paid more than $500,000 in cash for the construction and contents of the building. In years previous she wearied herself traveling to teach recruits. Now they could come to PORO to learn the fine arts of hair, skin, and nail care. Agents enjoyed a free week of classes every year. Students were taught every detail of how to walk, dress, and communicate. Annie knew them by name, and her interest in each generated a force of loyalty toward her.

She often worked at her desk beyond midnight and reappeared there just after dawn. As the business grew, she faced a common dilemma: Her time was stretched so thin that she could barely juggle all of the demands. A solution came in a most unexpected way.

Annie wasn't looking for a husband. In fact, she had already experienced divorce after a brief marriage during the early 1900s. But during a trip she met Aaron Malone, a former teacher turned traveling Bible salesman. He was persistent, and within two years they married. She appointed him operations manager and assigned him to handle daily interactions with business and political leaders. The strategy set her at a grave disadvantage that would haunt her in the future.

Although Annie founded her empire twenty years before, the 1920s stereotypical roles of men and women hampered her credibility once she had a husband. There were subtle examples of her apparent relinquishment of power, like when Aaron took credit for money that Annie donated. Then, at Wilberforce University, he was erroneously recognized during a public event "for his achievement in establishing and carrying on the great PORO College." Although Annie was in the audience, she did not correct the error, and neither did Aaron.

The pair argued about money, and Annie's wary inner circle considered Aaron an untrustworthy freeloader. Annie seemed to grant him all wishes to keep the peace, so she was blindsided when Aaron served her with divorce papers claming rights to 50 percent of the business. A massive public relations battle ensued. Annie appeared at a disadvantage for failing to correct the record to reflect that she was the owner of PORO.

The court battle for possession of PORO was tabloid fodder. Both of the Malones found themselves in the tenuous position of relinquishing the enterprise into the hands of a court-appointed receiver bent on changing the direction and philosophy of the company. Aaron finally agreed to the sum of $200,000 in cash and Annie retained the crippled business and hundreds of thousands of dollars in legal fees. Unfortunately, once the media published the details of her wealth, new lawsuits surfaced. Eventually the actions forced her to sell company property to raise money for the settlements.

Just a few years earlier, PORO had evolved toward greatness. Now Annie's dream lay wounded and things had changed dramatically. The company grossed only half a million dollars in 1929 as the nation faced the Great Depression. Two years before, in 1927, the immediate vicinity surrounding PORO College sustained massive damage during a tornado. And Annie felt hurt by many friends and associates who criticized her during the divorce. A new start was in order.

Chicago offered a fertile environment for a fresh beginning. In 1930, Annie acquired an impressive group of buildings on the city's south side, extending from Forty-Fourth to Forty-Fifth Streets along what is now Martin Luther King Drive. The four stately stone-and-brick structures featured turrets, mansard rooflines, and wide doorways rising from behind an impressive 6-foot wrought iron fence. The mansions looked more like private estates or a religious conclave than a company headquarters.

For a nominal fee, students pored over a wide array of subjects ranging from trimming hair to Marcel waving to beauty culture law. With PORO degrees recognized by national, state, and local boards, graduates left the hallowed halls confident of passing state board examinations. PORO agents were encouraged to enter contests to raise money for charity, with the grand prize being an all-expense-paid, fully chaperoned junket to PORO College.

Every Christmas Eve, Annie awarded employees with extravagant gifts. Those with five years of service were recognized with a diamond ring; gold went to those who bought a home during the year for themselves or their parents; money prizes were presented to those who were punctual, or maintained regular attendance, or proved good stewards of their personal savings. Some received once-in-a-lifetime vacations; others received a new home. Even those employees who remembered their raincoats, rubbers, and umbrellas during inclement weather were acknowledged with a bonus.

Civically, it is said she donated more than $33,000 during her lifetime to various YMCA facilities and, as a tribute to her parents, she built an orphanage for $10,000 and served as its president for nearly twenty-five years. Published reports indicate that she paid tuition for selected students attending black land-grant colleges and gifted over $25,000 to Howard University for medical research. Some called Annie a "freak giver," yet her extreme beneficence made her the largest financial contributor to African-American causes.

In return, four colleges conferred honorary degrees upon her. She was the only African-American woman given Life Member of the Woman's Christian Temperance Union, and, at the 1944 convention of the National Beauty Culturists League, her life was celebrated through a novel musical play. Annie humbly accepted a standing ovation that night, while hiding the worries she harbored.

PORO was being investigated for failure to comply with new tax rules for businesses selling luxury goods. By 1941, PORO was five years in arrears. Attempting to crush rumors of its impending demise, the company issued a statement hoping to clear its seventy-two-year-old founder. It explained, "Paid specialists are in charge of taxes and . . . therefore the head of a corporation has no reason for doubting the accuracy of those employed to handle such matters." The Chicago community mobilized to save the floundering company, but the $50,000 debt proved too much. Foreclosure was inevitable. Proceeds from the sale of company assets paid the bills. Annie spent her last years fretting over the fate of her cherished representatives.

When she died at age eighty-seven on May 10, 1957, at Chicago's Provident Hospital, it was widely reported that her wealth had shriveled to $100,000. While some historians report the fact as disappointing, Annie might have disagreed. Since she had no immediate family to which she could leave her fortune, her own words and actions indicate that she would have much rather spent every last cent on her PORO family than have any money remain beyond her life. As she wrote in a 1927 letter, "I think I could be no happier than giving service to my people and I am sure if I were forced or denied this privilege I would be terribly unhappy."

ir attire, and shoemakers pur-

ilt a comfortable fortune and
n splurged on a home for them
provided a retreat where they
animals.

s than the Europeans, so the
by performing in vaudeville
ade this foray into the follies a
es sacrificing their income for

dimentary guidelines regarding
umane treatment of show ani-
lthough animal inspectors vis-
ften overlooked if the trainer
matters worse, animal acts were

tage, audiences expected to see
riding on the backs of mon-
t happened when the curtain
o of them.

s door, the Castles often stum-
e dogs received after a show.
s, many were subjected to hav-
zzle, causing them to choke as
to look away.

for each dog. Without reserva-
amounts and rescued as many
ions were, this left them with
use them.

e on the street, searching for
It was exhausting and costly,

IRENE CASTLE

1893–1969

Humanitarian

SCORES OF DANCING ENTHUSIASTS GATHERED BENEATH the glittering crystal chandeliers of the Hotel Plaza's luxurious Grand Ballroom. Straining to catch a peek of America's First Lady of Ballroom Dancing, the crowd broke into boisterous applause when the lights dimmed and the spotlight followed an elegant elderly woman onto the dance floor.

Irene Castle graciously nodded her head in acknowledgment. Still a trendsetter at age seventy-one, she wore a custom designed gold and white brocade ball gown, with a ruffled princess neckline, and a dramatic train trimmed in pristine white fox. A tiara rested upon her trademark "Castle Bob" haircut.

Within moments she captivated the audience, swirling along in a graceful waltz. Irene lived in two wildly diverse worlds—one of celebrity and the other of charity. The wisdom of her life was that she used her celebrity to gain support for her causes.

Irene Foote was born on April 17, 1893, to Annie Elroy (Thomas) and Dr. Hubert Townsend Foote. The family lived on thirty-five acres in New Rochelle, New York. Irene considered her childhood idyllic, and cultivated romantic girlhood dreams of performing on stage.

New Rochelle attracted Broadway theater actors and moguls who vacationed there during the summer months. It was not uncommon to meet a matinee idol walking along the waterfront. That was exactly how she met Vernon (Blythe) Castle.

The native Englishman was a string bean of a man who performed comedy on Broadway. With Vernon's assistance, Irene earned a bit part on stage and, before long, fell in love with her champion. The round-faced, violet-eyed Irene became Mrs. Vernon Castle on May 28, 1911.

A new era began in March 1912, when the duo appeared as dance professionals for the first time in Paris, France. They danced in a stage review and at the Café de Paris, an exclusive club frequented by Russian royalty and wealthy socialites.

When the Castles seemingly floated onto the floor, the audience barely moved, their eyes transfixed on the young husband and wife gliding in and out of dances they'd created such as the Castle Walk, the Grizzly Bear, the Castle Polka, and the Fox Trot. The Castles settled into a lavish life supported by a commanding salary plus tips of diamonds and cash.

Irene was especially admired for her boyishly slim figure, high shoulders, and graceful hand movements. Although a teenager, Irene had an innate sense of style that changed the fashion world.

Not wanting to upstage the European clientele, she selected clean-looking, loose-fitting dresses with sparse decoration. The upper-crust women requested the name of her dressmaker.

The desire to imitate Irene soared into an international frenzy in 1914, when she cut her hair into a short crop that became popularly known as the "Castle Bob." Women also clamored for Irene's invention called the "Castle Band," which she wore pulled down over her forehead to hold her hair in place. The hairstyle became the defining look of the flapper era.

Photographs of Irene dominated magazines and newspapers.

Designers requested she model th
chased her image for advertising.

By 1915, the Castles had bu
decided to return to America. Vern
in Manhasset, New York. The estat
could rest and keep a menagerie of

Americans were less gratuito
Castles supplemented their incom
shows. There was one hitch that m
folly indeed, as they found themsel
animals featured in the show.

United States laws provided ru
the protection of animals, but the h
mals was not particularly enforced.
ited the theaters, infractions were
offered to spring for a beer. To make
extremely popular.

Oblivious to the suffering backs
tiny dogs jumping over barriers an
keys. Only a few people knew wh
closed, and Irene and Vernon were t

While exiting by the performer
bled onto the brutal punishments t
Besides beatings and shock treatment
ing a hose force water into their mu
liquid filled their lungs. Irene refused

She demanded a purchase price
tion, the couple paid the outrageous
dogs as possible. As gallant as their ac
armfuls of animals and no place to h

Desperately, they quizzed peopl
anyone who might desire a free dog

but nothing like what they would encounter when they heard a dreadful wailing from the basement of a theater.

The unfortunate creature housed in the dungeon-like recesses of Chicago's Palace Theater was a massive brown bear stuffed into a small cage. On stage the bear roller-skated around bottles, maneuvering tight figure eights while gently clutching a tiny poodle in his paws. During a photo shoot, Irene witnessed the bear's owner smash the unwitting beast with a baseball bat. Infuriated, Irene screamed, "How much do you want for the bear?"

Nine hundred dollars freed him. Finding him a home was another issue. After rejections from two zoos, Irene called Chicago's Lincoln Park Zoo. Initially, the manager declined, but later he offered to house the animal with a black bear. Thrilled, the Castles arranged for a taxi to drive them and their furry friend to the zoo. Unbeknownst to the cab driver, his patrons were not the typical paying customers.

The bear sat in the middle of the back seat with Irene and Vernon serving as bookends. Arriving at the gate, Vernon slid out of the car and rushed to retrieve zoo personnel while Irene remained as still as a statue, fearing that the bear would sense her vulnerability. The bear keeper safely coaxed the furry giant from the car, and the Castles managed to pull off one of their most daring rescues. It wouldn't be the last for Irene.

As World War I reached fever pitch, Vernon enlisted in the British Royal Air Force against Irene's wishes. On February 15, 1918, he perished while training a novice pilot.

Immediately upon Vernon's death, Irene found herself courted by eligible bachelors. Flattered by her suitors, she chose instead to keep busy. She wrote a book about Vernon titled *My Husband,* performed in silent films, granted interviews, and traveled.

She was photographed toting a bulldog in her arms and a lamb on a leash as she disembarked from the S.S. *Lafayette.* An interviewer noted Irene's devotions:

Mrs. Castle's two fads are babies and dogs. She maintains an orphanage in Manhasset and if she had her way, every unhappy dog in the world would find a home in her house.

Fourteen months after becoming a widow, Irene married Robert Treman, an Ithaca, New York, businessman. The marriage failed when Irene discovered Robert's shady business investments had bankrupted her.

Completely broke, Irene paired with dancer Billy Reardon and toured the nation, hoping to restore her financial independence. In Chicago, Irene accepted an invitation to dine with an old friend. The twist was that they would be hosted at the apartment of Chicago coffee tycoon and international polo player Major Frederic McLaughlin. The meal turned into a life-changing experience.

Fascinated by Irene's adamant refusal of a good-night kiss on that first encounter, Frederic announced on their second meeting that he intended to marry her. The third date, he proposed. After repartee as fast and demanding as the Quick Step, Irene agreed to consider his offer during her European tour.

After flip-flopping on the decision, Irene married Frederic in November 1923 and traded her dance career for the life of a socialite. Her concerns regarding the marriage turned out to be warranted.

Although Frederic loved Irene dearly, the twenty-one-year marriage proved to be a roller coaster of emotion. At one point they sued each other for divorce, but neither had the stomach for the court proceedings. They compromised by living in separate residences in Lake Forest, Illinois.

During calmer times, the McLaughlins shared many interests. Frederic purchased a hockey team, which he named the Chicago Blackhawks, and Irene collaborated by designing the team's jersey. Frederic accepted Irene's love of animals and permitted her to keep a veritable zoo, including a gorilla, an exotic meercat, monkeys, and a lion on the premises of their estate.

Irene fought the boredom of country club lunches and women's meetings. By 1928, a stir-crazy Irene was consumed with the idea of opening a shelter for stray and abandoned dogs.

A vacant ten-acre kennel in nearby Deerfield, Illinois, suited her vision. Using her own money, which she had earned from contracts modeling everything from hosiery to girdles, Irene financed the purchase, and, with friend Helen Swift, she began the repair and clean-up of the buildings.

In 1916, Irene was twirling in flowing chiffon and silk on Paris stages. Now, a dozen years later, she wore overalls and cotton shirts and spent hours on her hands and knees, scrubbing the floors of what would become a unique experiment in animal refuges.

The facility was named Orphans of the Storm after the 1921 film starring Lillian Gish. The movie ends with the reunion of sisters, and Irene hoped that the animals would enjoy the same fate.

Orphans of the Storm was the first shelter located outside of Chicago's city limits. On opening day, there still wasn't running water or electricity. Irene had a coal stove installed and covered the salary for an elderly caretaker to keep the main building heated. The office phone rang nonstop with requests to drop off or adopt a dog. Even the Chicago police asked her to accept their pound strays. The staggering demand caught Irene off guard, as did the failure of the property's well and the expense of a fence to secure the stream of animals that arrived daily.

Realizing the needs exceeded the funding, Irene turned to her contacts and wealthy friends for assistance. Movie stars provided testimonials, urging readers to donate generously to the project. Irene acted as interim veterinarian, and even as dogcatcher, duties which she accomplished from her Cadillac.

Placing animals into proper homes was paramount to Irene.

She drafted a unique contract, stating pets would be remanded into the care of a person yet remain the property of the shelter. Potential dog owners were subjected to careful scrutiny and agreed to a rigorous initial home inspection and unannounced follow-up visits. If conditions were below the contract standard, the dog could be forcibly taken back into the care of the shelter. This inspection process bloomed into another job for Irene.

Reports of animal abuse began flowing into the shelter. The county deputized Irene to conduct investigations and issue arrest warrants if animal cruelty was confirmed. Her focus broadened to the mistreatment of horses, cows, and pigs. When a farmer refused to correct violations, Irene took him to court.

The press loved photographing her descending the courthouse steps. Reporters noted the irony of her wearing fur and expensive jewelry as she testified against a "poor farmer." The images sold newspapers, especially when the verdict went against her. The laws exposed her to countersuits of slander. Wrapped in her cause, Irene ignored the strain that the courtroom put on her home life.

Irene knew the public considered her a crackpot. Some asked her why she didn't fight to protect children. Irene retorted, "The poor of the world have a thousand eloquent voices to speak for them besides tongues of their own."

Being a public figure, she was harassed with late-night telephone calls and threatening anonymous letters. She ignored the jokes, editorials, and personal attacks. Her obsession to protect animals clouded rational thinking when it came to her own well-being. Frederic's fear for his wife seemed valid when Orphans of the Storm burned to the ground.

Investigators failed to determine the origin of the fire. Irene refused to dwell on the potential that it was retribution for her activist positions. Undeterred, she pushed to rebuild and became even more vocal about animal rights. Her next battle would pit her against the medical community.

Irene uncovered a secret underworld of dog trafficking. Thieves earned income by heisting family pets and strays and selling them, no questions asked, to local medical schools for use in live animal experimentation. Irene countered by accepting stolen laboratory animals saved by sympathetic medical students, who smuggled them to her in clandestine meetings. From these interventions, Irene learned the horrific details of vivisection, the practice of using live animals for medical research and experimentation.

The practice infuriated her so much that she trespassed into the recovery laboratory at Northwestern University Medical School, scooped up a shaking toy collie from its cage, and rushed down the stairs to show its condition to reporters and the Chicago Health Commissioner.

As the daughter of a homeopathic doctor, she believed that nothing foreign, such as a serum, should be put into a human bloodstream. Confident that vaccination research was about money and not health, Irene offered herself as a human guinea pig, pledging $5,000 to any doctor who would allow her to be bitten by a rabid animal so that she could demonstrate that a rabies antidote was not needed.

No one took up her offer.

When the legislature passed a law requiring all dogs be vaccinated for rabies, Irene countered:

> A racket of vast scope and profit is the periodic rabies scares promoted through the assistance of city health departments. Although actual cases of deaths from rabies are almost unknown, millions of dollars are squandered annually by frightened persons on harmful and dangerous serums, through the connivance of dishonest health offices.

Irene took a leave of absence from the shelter and Chicago in 1938 in order to serve as an advisor in Hollywood on the film *The Story of Vernon and Irene Castle*. Cash donations to the shelter plummeted without her.

Upon her return Irene began fundraising fervently. She sponsored an annual Pooch Ball dinner dance and attended sporting events with Peter, a stately Saint Bernard who acted as the shelter's mascot and carried a leather purse on his collar where supporters could drop change. Irene answered photograph requests by providing a glossy eight by ten and a note asking for $1.00 to be donated to the Animal League. As she recovered from one crisis, she encountered another: Frederic died in 1944.

Three years later, Irene married George Enzinger, a Chicago advertising executive. Her declining health prompted doctors to recommend that she minimize her schedule. George suggested they winter in Arkansas. Suffering from emphysema, heart problems, and arthritis, Irene agreed to go.

While there, a for-sale sign caught their attention. The ten-acre peach farm featured a modest ranch home overlooking the stunning vistas of the Ozark Mountains. Best of all, when the front gates were closed, no one could get near them. They completed the transaction and began dividing time between Illinois and Arkansas. Meanwhile, with Irene away, a mutiny of sorts began brewing at Orphans of the Storm.

Irene returned to Illinois in June 1956, just as the staff resigned. The operation was in shambles and Irene made the gut-wrenching decision to humanely euthanize most of the dogs. Just as she had in the beginning, she took on all necessary jobs until new volunteers came forward. Grace Petkus accepted the paid position of managing director. Relieved, Irene felt confident that the shelter would survive without her daily involvement. Finally, she and George were free to enjoy their twilight years—or so they thought.

George died shortly after their move to Arkansas. Irene remained at their ranch, among the fruit trees, living with a personal secretary and a small bevy of dogs and cats from the shelter.

In 1965, an interviewer focused on Irene's life as a dancer. Irene corrected the writer, explaining that her will was drawn with orders to have her gravestone read, "Irene Castle—Humanitarian." She continued:

> Dancing was fun, and I needed the money, but Orphans of the Storm comes from the heart. It's more important.

Irene died of a stroke on January 25, 1969, at age seventy-six. She's buried where it all began, in New York, by Vernon's side.

In her autobiography *Castles in the Air* she wrote:

> It pains me to think that there is still so much to be done. It seems sometimes that we have barely started. But we have started, and "Orphans of the Storm" and what it stands for will survive me for a long, long time.

And so it does. Today, Orphans of the Storm animal shelter provides a safe harbor for strays and abandoned dogs and cats in the original northeastern Illinois location selected by Irene. Through this organization, thousands of needy pets have been placed into loving "forever homes."

RUTH PAGE

1899-1991

Ballet Pioneer

DESPITE THE BURNING HEAT RISING FROM the concrete streets of Chicago, and the risk of being mugged for the third time, eighty-year-old Ruth Page stepped confidently down the front stairs of her Lakeshore Avenue apartment building with fearless strides. Determined to complete her daily *barre,* she preferred to walk the five blocks to the Ruth Page Foundation Dance School, never considering the use of her personal fortune for a taxi or comfortable limousine ride to the school that bore her name. When the winter winds pushed the waves of Lake Michigan onto the sidewalks, Ruth rehearsed in the comfort of her home studio. If she didn't dance every day, she felt something was missing. She was a dancer to the very core of her being and often claimed that she was born dancing.

Ruth Marian Page entered the world on March 22, 1899. She was the middle child of three and the only daughter born to Dr. Lafayette and Marian Heinly Page. In her writings, Ruth described herself as "quite an ordinary, dark-haired, black-eyed baby born in an ordinary house in an ordinary town in the Middle West." Indeed, there was almost nothing ordinary about the Page family or their

RUTH PAGE

lifestyle. The thing that was most extraordinary about Ruth was that she didn't think her privileged upbringing was extraordinary at all.

Both of her parents were pillars of the community in Indianapolis, Indiana. Her father was a noted ear, nose, and throat specialist and surgeon who helped establish the James Whitcomb Riley Children's Hospital. Ruth's mother was an accomplished concert pianist, community activist, and cofounder of the Indianapolis Symphony Orchestra.

Education was paramount to Dr. and Mrs. Page, as was a life of routine and discipline. Morning breakfasts were peppered with poetry recitations; evenings included readings from the works of Tolstoy and Dickens; at bedtime the chords of Tchaikovsky, played by their mother, guided the children into sweet dreams. As a tot Ruth often accompanied her mother to their private music studio located in a separate building next to the main house. Ruth danced free form while her mother practiced. Around age eight Ruth set the goal of creating one new dance routine every day.

The Pages' estate served as a meeting place for politicians and artists, and it was not uncommon for performers to arrive after a show for conversation, refreshments, and, perhaps, an informal encore.

The first time Russian ballerina Anna Pavlova danced in Indianapolis, she took the city by storm. Although Ruth didn't attend the performance, she was mesmerized by everyone's vivid descriptions. She begged for formal training to become a toe dancer. Indianapolis offered many cultural advantages at the turn of the century, but training in formal ballet wasn't one of them. Her only recourse was to hound her dance teacher to order "toe clips" so that she could practice dancing *en point* on her own. She began years of self-imposed work with the intention of one day dancing with Pavlova.

During a return engagement of Anna Pavlova's dance company, fourteen-year-old Ruth was moved to tears. Afterward, Pavlova accepted an invitation to tea at the Page residence, and, learning of Ruth's interest in ballet, she requested that Ruth dance for her.

The seasoned Russian ballerina carefully studied Ruth's skills. Those early years of play dancing had negatively impacted Ruth's overall technique. However, Pavlova's philosophy was simple: "No one can arrive from being talented alone. Work transforms talent into genius." What Ruth lacked in technique, she'd demonstrated in desire, and Pavlova suggested Ruth train in Chicago with members of her corps.

In short order, Ruth became technically mature and was offered a position with Pavlova's company. Standing face to face with her golden opportunity, Ruth was quickly pulled back to earth by her mother, who agreed that she could accept Pavlova's offer only after completing school. It was nearly an unbearable compromise for the eager aspiring dancer. Fortunately, the place selected for Ruth's continuing education proved to be an advantage.

The New York City French School for Girls was deemed the hub of American culture and art. It's unclear whether or not Ruth's parents realized that the school directors would be quite sympathetic toward Ruth's passion. She enjoyed the freedom to maintain a rigorous practice schedule and the flexibility to perform at regular engagements. Finally, in 1918, Ruth packed her bags and began her journey into the world of dance, later explaining, "At an early age I felt the need to soar, to dream, to fly away."

Traveling as a member of Pavlova's company, Ruth was introduced to the harsh facts of a ballet dancer's life. Since Russia was considered the pinnacle of ballet, the first order of business was to change her name from Ruth Page to the more Russian-sounding Natasha Stepanova. Ruth gladly became a wide-eyed, dedicated member of the dance chorus, which she affectionately labeled the "Pavlovitas."

The bouncy teenager, who was properly chaperoned by her mother, willingly accepted the long hours and grueling daily schedule.

She never complained about the required early morning barre exercises followed by three hours of warm-up. Before performances, Ruth promptly donned her costume, arranged her hair, and carefully applied resin to her toe shoes. When the stage director called the dancers to assume their positions, Ruth was already standing in the wings, anxious for the music that signaled her entrance into the footlights.

After each performance of delicate femininity, she joined her comrades on the hunt for a suitable restaurant, where they would ravenously wolf down a meal of thick steaks. After dining, she retired to soak in a hot bath to soothe her sore muscles and the bruises accidentally pressed into her ribs by the fingers of her male dance partners.

As a novice, Ruth found that first tour quite glamorous and exciting even as she dragged her luggage between trains and ships. It was the beginning of her seventy years of travel throughout North and South America, Europe, and Asia. Her life became a whirlwind of memories with photographic evidence of her walks along Moscow streets and French beaches and through Japanese temples. When one tour ended, another began. As testament to her talent, Ruth never suffered the rejection of a failed audition—she always got the job.

Of course, connections didn't hurt either. A former teacher, Adolph Bolm, invited Ruth to Chicago to dance the lead role in his 1919 production of *The Birthday of the Infanta*. The prima ballerina didn't fail her mentor. The morning after the premiere, critics gushed over the "unknown" twenty-year-old American ballerina named Ruth Page. "Where has she been?" one critic asked. Another raved that Ruth was "perfect in the role." Ruth joked years later that she read the reviews and thought to herself that it was so easy to have a career in dance. With self-deprecating humor, she mused, "I have of course been going down, down, down ever since!" On the contrary, her career was going up and up.

From 1922 to 1924, Ruth was the only ballerina contracted to dance in Irving Berlin's *Music Box Review*. The following year she became the first American to perform with Russia's Diaghilev's Ballet Russe, then the ballet director for the Ravinia Festival Opera for two seasons while simultaneously appearing as the premiere danseuse with the Chicago-based Allied Arts Ballet. And the offers continued.

The Metropolitan Opera of New York selected her as its first American ballet soloist. Her feet were heralded as the "world's most beautiful" in an advertising campaign for ballet shoes. She became the first dancer to appear in a movie that synchronized recorded music to her movements on film.

Ruth was seemingly comfortable in every situation. She danced for royalty, dignitaries, and wealthy patrons. In 1928 she performed during the coronation of Japan's Emperor Hirohito and later wrote of it with casualness and calm.

While on the road, Ruth was showered with flowers, letters, and jewelry from interested gentlemen. Closer to home, two young men especially caught her attention and alarmed her mother. Ruth attempted to quell Marian's fears by clarifying that she liked both young men very much, but she liked her dancing even more. Recalling that she had sacrificed her own musical career to be a traditional wife and mother, Marian urged Ruth to stay focused on dance, responding,

With his clear legal mind, he should be able to see that your work means exactly to you just what his work means to him. He could not possibly imagine himself giving up his work on account of marriage, and no mere man can understand that it is possible for a woman's work to be as much a part of herself as a man's work is of himself. We are living in a transition stage and you are a pioneer!

By the time her mother's advice arrived, Ruth found herself smitten by another young man whom, she soon realized, she liked as much as her dancing. Ruth made a fateful decision dictated by her heart when in 1925 she married Thomas Hart Fisher, a dashing, Harvard-educated Chicago lawyer and secretary of the Chicago Allied Arts.

As was common for that era, the wedding ceremony was conducted in the spacious living room of her parents' Indianapolis home. Uncommonly though, Ruth refused to adopt Tom's last name as hers, explaining that retaining the Page name was in the best interest of her career. This was just the beginning act of a rather unconventional forty-four-year marriage.

During their Monte Carlo honeymoon, Tom learned another lesson about being the husband of a ballerina. Days that should have been spent in new marital bliss were sacrificed as Ruth rushed off to classes with Italian dance master Enrico Cecchetti. And, within days of their arrival, choreographer Sergei Diaghilev called to employ her immediately for his European tour, cutting further into Tom's hopes of enjoying time with his bride.

Realizing Ruth was in her element, Tom gallantly arranged for her mother to join her while he returned to work in the United States. Years later, Ruth teased that as a result of this early experience, her "husband was trained right away." At first blush, it seemed as though she might always get her way. However, the union caused one stumbling block that, professionally, Ruth would never overcome.

Marriage to Tom Fisher of Chicago meant the couple would live in the Windy City. The idea caused Ruth anxiety. New York City was the indisputable cultural mecca of the United States; the best dancers and teachers lived and performed there. She knew a permanent residence in Chicago was a sacrifice that could have a dire impact on her career.

Ruth's fears had merit. New York City theater agents bluntly advised her that if she didn't drop the name Chicago from her ballet company, they would not be able to sell tickets. Toward the end of her life, critics wrote that had she stayed in New York City, she would have shared the same spotlight and stardom as her American dance contemporaries Martha Graham and Agnes de Mille.

Arguing over a home base was not high on Ruth's list. The world of dance was on the brink of a revolution, and Ruth was standing at the forefront. In 1925, she was the first artist to commission George Balanchine to create a dance for her. She also felt the call to choreograph for others.

Drifting from the strict formula of French and Russian ballet, Ruth used subjects that reflected American topics and lifestyles. In 1926, Ruth premiered a ballet titled *The Flapper and the Quarterback*. The dance portrayed a couple of lighthearted teenagers living large during the Roaring Twenties, and introduced American audiences to a fresh and contemporary example of the pas de deux, which is a dance for just two performers.

Ruth discovered she had the ability to visualize a ballet from beginning to end. Once she selected a topic, she formulated the dance steps, costumes, backdrops, and concept in her mind and then set about to find artists, dancers, and costumers to create her vision.

At the 1933 Century of Progress World's Fair in Chicago, Ruth challenged the boundaries of race and prejudice by choreographing a freestyle ballet titled *La Guiablesse,* in which she danced the role of a white woman demon and shared the stage with a corps of fifty-five African-American dancers. This revolutionary dance propelled the career of Katherine Dunham, the nation's first African-American ballerina.

Ruth flirted with feminism in 1937 with *An American Pattern,* touching on women's issues that wouldn't be discussed openly until the 1960s. And audiences were surprised when dancers in two of Ruth's ballets spoke their parts while dancing sans music. For the ballet *Hear Ye! Hear Ye!* she paid $150 for an original musical score from an unknown composer named Aaron Copland.

In the middle of her creative fervor, the country fell into the throes of the Great Depression. President Franklin D. Roosevelt's New Deal provided federally funded jobs for workers through the Works Progress Administration (WPA). The Dance Project was an offshoot of the WPA Federal Theatre Project. Ruth Page and choreographer Bentley Stone accepted positions with the Chicago WPA. In 1938 Ruth and Bentley collaborated on the ballet *Frankie and Johnny.* Based on a risqué bar song with themes of infidelity and murder, the plot was unconventional and risky, and so was Ruth's choreography. Ruth was not driven by hot topics to fill theater seats, and yet some of her dances were too hot for audiences.

Around this time Ruth produced the genre that would become her trademark: the opera ballet. Her first offering, *Guns and Castanets,* was based on the opera *Carmen.* Although it was interpretive dance, Ruth knew instinctively that it wasn't necessary to act out each word.

After the WPA ended, Ruth focused on modern dance. Her desire to intrigue audiences with only movement led her to artist and designer Isamu Noguchi. Together they developed sack-like costumes that were sculptural, ethereal, and visually fascinating. The sacks were used in her critically acclaimed ballet *Expanding Universe.*

Ruth managed to pull off a coup d'état in 1962, when she snagged the Russian defector Rudolf Nureyev to dance his first performance on American soil as a member of her Ruth Page Chicago Opera Ballet. She loved the delicious irony that the show was in New York.

In 1965, Ruth was recruited to choreograph and direct *The Nutcracker* at Chicago's Arie Crown Theater. Not everyone was thrilled with her appointment. Knowledge of her unusual and provocative productions raised the ire of some. There was snide whispering that she might have the nutcracker dance in psychedelic surroundings and conclude with him landing on the moon. Always unpredictable, Ruth did the most unpredictable thing of all.

The first day of rehearsal, Ruth assigned step combinations that were standard for *The Nutcracker* ballet. The adult dancers, who knew Ruth well, were quite stunned. When questioned about her conservative approach, she responded, "Darling, we're doing a classical ballet here. This isn't a Ruth Page ballet! It demands we do it a certain way."

While Ruth was directing *The Nutcracker,* Tom was suffering from ill health. In business, the pair had emerged as dynamos. Over the years they'd settled into a routine where she toured for nine months and then joined him for three months of entertaining as Mrs. Tom Fisher. When they were apart, they wrote one another virtually every day. His pet name for her was "Peter" after the character Peter Pan, and when he called her that, she was reduced to girl-like giggles. Again, unconventional for the times, they never had children.

For Ruth, her dancers were the children she never bore. In the 1970s, she wistfully confessed in her diary that she wished that Larry Long, who was her student and later director of her school, had been her son. And yet, she was aloof. Larry Long told an interviewer that for her entire life he called her Miss Page.

When it came to emotions, even her beloved Tom was held at arm's length. This was a woman who demonstrated her passion, loss, laughter, and pain through dance. In an interview she apologized for her inability to verbally express her feelings:

> I know that you would like to have me tell you all my innermost
> feelings, my profound emotions about all the things that hap-
> pened to me in my life. But, I tell you I never tell anybody. I tend
> to keep them to myself. . . . I'm sorry not to be able to.

She did share poignant moments in her diary as she worked through the grief and anxiety she felt when Tom began suffering unusual symptoms. Puzzled doctors offered no treatments or hope of recovery. By Ruth's description, Tom was withering away, and in desperation, she recorded her honest and wrenching thoughts: "Tom is dying. I wish I could die with him."

Even facing death, the two worked as a team. From his hospital bed, Tom started the necessary legal arrangements to form a dance school that would carry on Ruth's legacy. Their love story ended in 1969, when Tom lost his battle with Lou Gehrig's disease. Ruth honored his memory by throwing a party at their Chicago apartment. Later she declared it "one of the most interesting parties I have ever attended."

Tom's passing began a new chapter for Ruth. She unapologetically threw herself into fundraising for dance projects. Once she disgustedly challenged a board of directors with her favorite phrase: "Be adventuresome—be chic!" If a child showed any inkling of interest in dance, she personally awarded him or her a scholarship to attend classes at the Ruth Page Foundation.

While some dancers might bemoan the loss of physical strength and performance ability, Ruth relished the prospect of growing older. Upon accepting the 1980 *Dance Magazine* Award, she quipped that being eighty was "absolutely the most fun I've ever had in my life."

At the sprightly age of eighty-five, she married her long-time friend and artistic collaborator of twenty-three years, Andre Delfau. It was Delfau's paintings of ballerinas on the walls of Ruth's avant-garde apartment that so impressed visitors. In the late 1980s, Ruth's regular presence at her dance school diminished as did her public appearances. In her waning years she lost her ability to walk, but her mind was ever present in thoughts of dancing.

On April 7, 1991, ninety-two-year-old Ruth Page died of respiratory failure in her Chicago Lakeshore apartment. Obituaries repeatedly called her a dance pioneer. Ironically, her passing was eclipsed by the loss of two other dance icons: Ballerina Dame Margot Fonteyn died seven weeks before Ruth, and one of Ruth's contemporary competitors in the field of modern dance, Martha Graham, passed away on April 1, 1991.

Ruth is buried at Chicago's Graceland Cemetery. Her resting place is marked with a striking monument bearing merely her name, the years of her birth and death, and an etched image of artist Isamu Noguchi's *Expanding Universe*. The leaping figure is draped in Ruth's favorite sculptural costume, stretching earnestly toward the sky.

Ruth wrote these wistful words in her 1938 diary:

I was a child with longings for the moon, and I could never be happy because I never even came within reach of it.

Of course, she could not possibly touch the moon. But at the end of her life, she had attained her closest proximity as she was heralded by her peers as a ballet star.

BIBLIOGRAPHY

Christiana Holmes Tillson

Brush, Daniel H. *Growing Up with Southern Illinois: The Pioneer Memoirs of Daniel H. Brush.* Chicago: The Lakeside Press, R. R. Donnelley and Sons Company, 1944.

Carr, Kay J. Introduction to *A Woman's Story of Pioneer Illinois* by Christiana Holmes Tillson. Carbondale: Southern Illinois University Press, 1995.

Collins, William H., and Cicero F. Perry. *Past and Present of the City of Quincy and Adams County, Illinois.* Chicago: The S. J. Clarke Publishing Company, 1905.

Faragher, John Mack. *Sugar Creek: Life on the Illinois Prairie.* New Haven, Conn.: Yale University Press, 1986.

The History of Adams County, Illinois. Chicago: Murray, Williamson and Phelps, 1879.

Saxon, Martha. *Being Good: Women's Moral Values in Early America.* New York: Hill and Wang, 2003.

Strange, A. T. "John Tillson," *The Journal of the Illinois State Historical Society* XVII, no. 4 (January 1925): 715–23.

Tillson, Christiana Holmes. *A Woman's Story of Pioneer Illinois.* Milo Milton Quaife, ed. Chicago: The Lakeside Press, R. R. Donnelley and Sons Company, 1919.

Anna Elizabeth Slough

Bateman, Newton, and Paul Selby, eds. *Historical Encyclopedia of Illinois,* vol.1. Chicago: Munsell Publishing Company, 1901.

Bess, F. B. *Eine Populäre Geschichte der stadt Peoria.* Peoria, Ill.: W. H. Wagner and Sons, 1906.

Davis, James E. *Frontier Illinois.* Bloomington: Indiana University Press, 1998.

The History of Peoria County, Illinois. Chicago: Johnson and Company, 1880: 780–81.

McCulloch, David, ed. *History of Peoria County,* vol. 2. Peoria, Ill.: Munsell Publishing Company, 1902: 298.

Emma Hale Smith

Arrington, Leonard J., Feramorz Y. Fox, and Dean L. May. *Building the City of God: Community and Cooperation among the Mormons.* Salt Lake City, Utah: Deseret Book Company, 1976; reprint, Urbana: University of Illinois Press, 1992.

Blum, Ida. *Nauvoo—Gateway to the West.* Carthage, Ill.: Journal Printing Company, 1974.

Givens, George W. *In Old Nauvoo: Everyday Life in the City of Joseph.* Salt Lake City, Utah: Deseret Book Company, 1990.

History of Relief Society, 1842–1966. Salt Lake City, Utah: The General Board of Relief Society, 1966.

Holzapfel, Richard Neitzel, and Jeni Broberg Holzapfel. *Women of Nauvoo.* Salt Lake City, Utah: Bookcraft, Inc., 1992.

Hurd, Jerrie W. *Our Sisters in the Latter-Day Scriptures.* Salt Lake City, Utah: Deseret Book Company, 1987.

Jones, Gracia N. *Emma's Glory and Sacrifice: A Testimony.* Hurricane, Utah: Homestead Publishers and Distributors, 1987.

———. *Emma and Joseph: Their Divine Mission.* American Fork, Utah: Covenant Communications, 1999.

Miller, David E., and Della S. Miller. *Nauvoo: The City of Joseph.* Santa Barbara, Calif.: Peregrine Smith, Inc., 1974.

Newell, Linda King, and Valeen Tippetts Avery. *Mormon Enigma: Emma Hale Smith, Prophet's Wife, "Elect Lady," Polygamy's Foe.* Garden City, N.Y.: Doubleday & Company, Inc., 1984.

Terry, Keith, and Ann Terry. *Emma: The Dramatic Biography of Emma Smith.* Santa Barbara, Calif.: Butterfly Publishing, Inc., 1979.

Youngreen, Buddy. *Reflections of Emma: Joseph Smith's Wife.* Orem, Utah: Grandin Book Company, 1994.

Lydia Moss Bradley

Bible Records, provided by Mrs. A. V. Danner, reprinted in the *Switzerland Democrat,* December 13, 1928. Originally from the *Indianapolis Star,* date unknown. Photocopied, Peoria Historical Society Collection, Bradley University Library, Peoria, Ill.

Codicil No. 2, Last Will and Testament of Lydia Moss Bradley, December 31, 1897. Peoria, Ill. Photocopy, Special Collections Center, Bradley University Library, Peoria, Ill.

Hammond, W. W. "Review of Mrs. Bradley's Life and Business," Private journal, January 1908. Photocopy, Special Collections Center, Bradley University Library, Peoria, Ill.

Lydia Moss Bradley Papers, Peoria Historical Society Collection, Bradley University Library, Peoria, Ill.

"Mrs. Lydia Bradley," Photocopy, *The Tech,* vol. 1, no. 1 (February 1898):1–3.

IRENE CASTLE

THIS BUILDING IS DEDICATED
to
THE LOVING MEMORY OF

ELEPHANT   GRETCHEN
NELLIE   BROWNIE
PIPPS   GIRLIE
MARY   ANNA
JIM   TEE

AND
THE MANY OTHER FAITHFUL FRIENDS
WHO PERISHED BY FIRE
FEBRUARY 1930

Shriner Scrapbook, 1885–1900: Peoria, Ill., 1900. Photocopy, Special Collections Center, Bradley University Library, Peoria, Ill.

The Switzerland County Historical Society. "Highlights of Switzerland County History," Vevay, Ind.

Upton, Allen A. *Forgotten Angel: The Story of Lydia Moss Bradley.* The United States of America: Allen A. Upton, copyright, 1988, 1994.

Wyckoff, Charles Truman, ed. *Bradley Polytechnic Institute: The First Decade, 1897–1907.* Peoria, Ill.: Bradley Polytechnic Institute, 1908.

Yates, Louis A. R. *A Proud Heritage: Bradley's History, 1897–1972.* Peoria, Ill.: Bradley University, Observer Press, 1974.

———. "Lydia Moss Grave Rededication," June 18, 1980. Photocopy, Special Collections Center, Bradley University Library, Peoria, Ill.

Candace McCormick Reed

Advertisements as appeared in the *Quincy Whig* and the *Daily Whig Republican,* 1859–1887. Quincy Library Archives. Quincy, Ill.

Davis, William C. "A Spirit in My Feet," *Civil War Times,* vol. 21, no. 2 (April 1982): 8–17.

"Death of Mrs. Reed," Quincy (Illinois) *Daily Whig,* April 8, 1900.

"Fire," *Quincy Daily Herald,* November 28, 1878.

The History of Adams County, Illinois. Chicago: Murray, Williamson and Phelps, 1879.

"Honored Life Is Now Ended," *Quincy Daily Herald,* April 9, 1900.

Landrum, Carl. "Reed Photos Record Early Years," *Quincy Herald-Whig,* May 16, 1982, 4E.

———. "Reed Studio Recorded Scenes of Early Quincy," *Quincy Herald-Whig,* April 18, 1993.

———. "Photo Recalls Quincy of 1848," *Quincy Herald-Whig,* September 26, 1965, 3C.

———. "From Quincy's Past: Photographers Were Here in 1840s," *Quincy Herald-Whig,* July 7, 1968.

Landrum, Carl, and Shirley Landrum. *Quincy, Illinois.* Chicago: Arcadia Publishing, 2000.

"The Man about Town," *Quincy Daily Whig,* January 12, 1890, 4,11.

Massey, Mary Elizabeth. *Women in the Civil War.* Lincoln: University of Nebraska, 1994.

Murphy, Lucy Eldersveld, and Wendy Hamand Venet, eds. *Midwestern Women: Work, Community, and Leadership at the Crossroads.* Bloomington: Indiana University Press, 1997.

Nelson, Iris. "Introduction to Women at Work," Illinois Women at Work Project, September 24, 1999. Alliance Library System with the Historical Society of Quincy and Adams County, Quincy, Illinois. http://history.alliancelibrarysystem.com/Illinois Women/work.cfm.

———. "The Best Light in Town," *STARadio WomenSpeak,* Fall 2001, 77–79.

Palmquist, Peter. "Women Artists of the American West: Women in Photography Archive." http://www.sla.purdue.edu/WAAW/Palmquist/Essays.htm.

"Tossed from a Truck," *Quincy Weekly Whig,* December 5, 1878.

Mary Todd Lincoln

Baker, Jean H. *Mary Todd Lincoln: A Biography.* New York: W. W. Norton and Company, 1987.

Bolden, Tonya. *The Book of African-American Women: 150 Crusaders, Creators, and Uplifters.* Cincinnati, Ohio: Adams Media Corporation, 1997.

Fleishner, Jennifer. *Mrs. Lincoln and Mrs. Keckly: The Remarkable Story of the Friendship between a First Lady and a Former Slave.* New York: Broadway Books, 2003.

Friedman, Jane M. *America's First Woman Lawyer: The Biography of Myra Bradwell.* Buffalo, N.Y.: Prometheus Books, 1993.

Grubin, David, and Geoffrey C. Ward. "Abraham and Mary Lincoln: A House Divided." DVD. *The American Experience,* the History Channel. Los Angeles: Paramount Home Video, 2001.

Guillory, Dan. "Courtship and Politics: Lincoln and Douglas as Suitors," *Illinois Heritage,* A Publication of the Illinois State Historical Society, vol. 7, no. 1, January–February 2004: 10–13.

Keckley, Elizabeth. *Behind the Scenes: Thirty Years a Slave, and Four Years in the White House.* New York: 1868; reprint, Arno Press and the *New York Times,* 1968.

Kunhardt, Dorothy Meserve, and Philip B. Kunhardt Jr. *Twenty Days.* New York: Harper and Row Publisher, Inc., 1965.

Morrow, Honore Willsie. *Mary Todd Lincoln: An Appreciation of the Wife of Abraham Lincoln.* New York: William Morrow and Company, 1928.

Neely, Jr., Mark E., and R. Gerald McMurtry. *The Insanity File: The Case of Mary Todd Lincoln.* Carbondale: Southern Illinois University, 1986.

Rogers, Curtis E. "Elizabeth Keckley Behind the Scenes: A Memoir." MasterBuy Audiobook, 1996.

Sandburg, Carl. *Mary Lincoln: Wife and Widow.* New York: Harcourt, Brace and Company, Inc., 1932.

Turner, Justin G., and Linda Levitt Turner. *Mary Todd Lincoln: Her Life and Letters.* New York: Alfred A. Knopf, 1972.

VanderHeuvel, Gerry. *Crowns of Thorns and Glory: Mary Todd Lincoln and Varina Howell Davies: The Two First Ladies of the Civil War.* New York: E. P. Dutton, 1988.

Myra Bradwell

Berry, Dawn Bradley. *The 50 Most Influential Women in American Law.* Los Angeles: Lowell House, RGA Publishing Group, 1996.

Friedman, Jane M. *America's First Woman Lawyer: The Biography of Myra Bradwell.* Buffalo, N.Y.: Prometheus Books, 1993.

Morello, Karen Berger. *The Woman Lawyer in America, 1638 to the Present: The Invisible Bar.* New York: Random House, 1986.

Wheaton, Elizabeth. *Myra Bradwell: First Woman Lawyer.* Greensboro, N.C.: Morgan Reynolds, Inc., 1997.

Dr. Ella Flagg Young

Blount, Jackie M. *Destined to Rule the Schools: Women and the Superintendency, 1873–1995.* Albany, N.Y.: SUNY Press, 1998.

"Ella Flagg Young Dies in Service of Her Country," *Illinois State Historical Society Journal* 11 (1918): 654–56.

Evans, John. "A Woman at the Head," *The Outlook Illustrated* 93, no. 4 (September 25, 1909): 180–81.

Herrick, Mary J. *The Chicago Schools: A Social and Political History.* Beverly Hills, Calif.: Sage Publications, 1971.

Johnson, Henry C., and Erwin V. Johanningmeier. *Teachers for the Prairie: The University of Illinois and the Schools, 1868–1945.* Champagne Urbana: University of Illinois Press, 1972.

McMannis, John T. *Ella Flagg Young and a Half-Century of the Chicago Public Schools.* Chicago: A. C. McClurg & Company, 1916.

Mead, George Herbert. "A Heckling School Board and an Educational Stateswoman," Survey 31, 1914: 443–44.

Smith, Joan K. *Ella Flagg Young: Portrait of a Leader.* Ames: Educational Studies Press and the Iowa State University Research Foundation, 1976, 1979.

Young, Dr. Ella Flagg. *Isolation in the School*. Chicago: University of Chicago Press, 1900.

————. "Scientific Method in Education," Decennial Publications of the University of Chicago, First Series, 3 (1903): 143–55.

Jane Addams

Addams, Jane. *A Centennial Reader*. New York: The MacMillan Company, 1960.

————. *Twenty Years at Hull-House*. New York: The MacMillan Company, 1916; reprint, Signet Classic/Penguin Putnam, Inc., 1961.

————. *Second Twenty Years at Hull-House*. New York: The MacMillan Company, 1930.

————. *The Long Road of Woman's Memory*. New York: The MacMillan Company, 1916; reprint, Urbana: University of Illinois Press, reprint, 2002.

Brown, Victoria. *The Education of Jane Addams*. Philadelphia: University of Pennsylvania Press, 2004.

Davis, Allen F. *American Heroine: The Life and Legend of Jane Addams*. New York: Oxford University Press, 1973.

Diliberto, Gioia. *A Useful Woman: The Early Life of Jane Addams*. New York: A Lisa Drew Book/Scribner, 1999.

Elshtain, Jean Bethke. *Jane Addams and the Dream of American Democracy*. New York: Basic Books, 2002.

Elshtain, Jean Bethke, ed. *The Jane Addams Reader*. New York: Basic Books, 2002.

Linn, James Weber. *Jane Addams: A Biography*. New York: D. Appleton-Century Company, 1936; reprint, Urbana: University of Illinois Press, 2000.

Meigs, Cornelia. *Jane Addams: Pioneer for Social Justice*. Boston: Little, Brown and Company, 1970.

Polikoff, Barbara Garland. *With One Bold Act: The Story of Jane Addams*. Chicago: Boswell Books, 1999.

Annie Minerva Turnbo Pope Malone

Bolden, Tonya. *The Book of African-American Women: 150 Crusaders, Creators, and Uplifters*. Holbrook, Mass.: Adams Media Corporation, 1996.

Bundles, A'Lelia. *On Her Own Ground: The Life and Times of Madam C. J. Walker*. New York: Simon and Schuster, 2001.

Byrd, Ayana D., and Lori L. Tharps. *Hair Story: Untangling the Roots of Black Hair in America*. New York: St. Martin's Press, 2001.

Claude Barnett Files. Photocopied, Special Collections, Chicago Historical Society, Chicago, Ill.

Kremer, Gary R., and Antonio F. Holland. *Missouri's Black Heritage*. Columbia: University of Missouri Press, 1993.

Peiss, Kathy. *Hope in a Jar: The Making of American's Beauty Culture*. New York: Metropolitan Books, Henry Holt and Company, 1998.

Porter, Gladys, L. *Three Negro Pioneers in Beauty Culture*. New York: Vantage Press, 1966.

Silverman, Robert Mark. "The Effects of Racism and Racial Discrimination on Minority Business Development: The Case of Black Manufacturers in Chicago's Ethnic Beauty Aids Industry," *Journal of Social History,* vol. 31 (Spring 1998): 571–97.

Smith, Jessie Carney. *Epic Lives: One Hundred Black Women Who Made a Difference*. Detroit, Mich.: Visible Ink Press, 1993.

Wilkerson, J. L. *Story of Pride, Power and Uplift: Annie T. Malone*. Kansas City, Miss.: Acorn Books, 2003.

Irene Castle

Adler, Barbara Squier. "Then and Now: Irene Castle," *New York Times,* December 10, 1950: 42.

Arey, Dr. Leslie B. to Frederick J. Nachman at the Chicago Historical Society, 26 January 1975. Irene Castle (McLaughlin, Enzinger) file, Chicago Historical Society.

Carson, Gerald. "In Chicago: Cruelty and Kindness to Animals," *Chicago History,* vol. 3, no. 3, Winter, 1974–1975: 151–58.

Castle, Irene. *Castles in the Air.* Garden City, N.Y.: Doubleday and Company, 1958.

———. *My Husband.* New York: Charles Scribner's Sons, 1919.

———. *Orphans of the Storm Year Book, 1939–40.* Deerfield, Ill., 1940.

———. *Orphans of the Storm Year Book, 1946–47.* Deerfield, Ill., 1947.

———. *Orphans of the Storm Year Book, 1956.* Deerfield, Ill., 1956.

———. *Orphans of the Storm Year Book, 1957.* Deerfield, Ill., 1957.

Duncan, Donald. "Irene Castle in 1956," *Dance Magazine,* vol. 30 (October 1956): 87–89.

———. "Irene Castle, 'Comeback,'" *Dance Magazine,* vol. 32 (March 1958): 74.

Eskil, Ragna B., and Irene Castle McLaughlin. "Is Vivisection Inhumane? A Debate," *The Forum,* vol. 93 (1942): 213–17.

"Happy Birthday to Irene Castle," *Ballroom Dance Magazine,* vol. 5, no. 3 (March 1964): 4–5.

"Irene Castle Packing Up," *Chicago Sun Times,* October 13, 1954.

"Irene Castle, Dancer, Dies at 75," *New York Times,* Sec. 1, January 26, 1969: 72.

"Irene Castle Honored at 'America's Ball of the Year,'" *Ballroom Dance Magazine,* vol. 5, no. 5 (May 1964): 4–10.

Naylor, Hazel Simpson. "A Castle 'Over There,'" *Motion Picture Magazine,* vol. 117, no. 5 (June 1919): 32–34.

"Orphans of the Storm Founder Dies," *Deerfield Review,* January, 29, 1969.

Terhune, Albert Payson. "Gone to the Dogs," *Good Housekeeping,* vol. 95 (November 1932): 34, 132–34.

"They Stand Out from the Crowd," *Literary Digest,* vol. 116, July 29, 1933: 9.

Treman, Irene Castle. "I Bobbed My Hair and Then…," *The Ladies Home Journal,* vol. 38 (October 1921): 124.

William McLaughlin, interviewed by Lyndee J. Henderson, 2000, author's collection.

Ruth Page

Anderson, Jack. "Ruth Page, Dancer, Is Dead at 92; Proudly American Choreographer." *New York Times,* April 9, 1991.

Barzel, Ann. "Ruth Page," *Dance Magazine,* vol. 65 (August 1991): 26–27.

"Dance Magazine Awards '80," transcript of event, *Dance Magazine,* vol. 54 (July 1980): 48–56.

Goodman, Saul. "Ruth Page: Cosmopolite of the Central Plains," *Dance Magazine,* vol. 35 (December 1961): 40–47.

———. "Ruth Page Discusses Opera-into-Ballet," *Dance Magazine,* vol. 35, no. 24 (February 1961): 24, 26–27, 62–63.

Gordon, Lon. "The Centennial Celebration Monograph: 1889–1999; A Life of Firsts." Ruth Page Center for the Arts. www.ruthpage.org/About%20Us/History.asp.

Martin, John. *Ruth Page: An Intimate Biography.* New York: Marcel Dekker, Inc., 1977.

Page, Ruth. Class: *Notes on Dance Classes around the World, 1915-1980,* Andrew Mark Wentink, ed. Princeton, N.J.: Princeton Book Company, 1984.

————. *Page by Page.* Andrew Mark Wentink, ed. Brooklyn, N.Y.: Dance Horizons, 1978.

————. "We Who Travel," *Dance Magazine,* vol. 41 (June 1967): 62, 82–83.

Silberstein, Scott. "Longings for the Moon: The Real Ruth Page." VHS. *Chicago Stories,* WTTW's Network Chicago. Chicago, Ill.: HMS Media, November 2000.

Smith, Cecil. "Dance: The Vipers of Paris," *New Republic,* vol. 122 (May 29, 1950): 21–22.

ABOUT THE AUTHOR

Lyndee Jobe Henderson has been digging up history, literally, ever since she was a little girl accompanying her father on archeological expeditions. The courage of ordinary people living in extraordinary times impressed this Johnstown, Pennsylvania, native, who grew up hearing stories and reading about the 1889 Johnstown Flood.

Illinois history has been Lyndee's passion for twenty-five years, ever since moving to Chicago's western suburbs. She has studied Mary Todd Lincoln and the roles of women during the Civil War and lectured and written about prairie life, the language of flowers, and Victorian wedding customs. This is her third book.

As the mom of two grown children, she shares her empty nest with her husband and three tiny fluff-ball Pomeranians that jockey to supervise the writer's life from Lyndee's lap.